The Rainy Day Toddler Activity Book

The
Rainy Day Toddler
Activity Book

100+ Fun Early Learning Activities
for Inside Play

Krissy Bonning-Gould

Illustrations by Natascha Rosenberg

ROCKRIDGE PRESS

Copyright © 2019 by Rockridge Press, Emeryville, California

No part of this publication may be reproduced, stored in a retrieval system, or transmitted in any form or by any means, electronic, mechanical, photocopying, recording, scanning, or otherwise, except as permitted under Sections 107 or 108 of the 1976 United States Copyright Act, without the prior written permission of the Publisher. Requests to the Publisher for permission should be addressed to the Permissions Department, Rockridge Press, 6005 Shellmound Street, Suite 175, Emeryville, CA 94608.

Limit of Liability/Disclaimer of Warranty: The Publisher and the author make no representations or warranties with respect to the accuracy or completeness of the contents of this work and specifically disclaim all warranties, including without limitation warranties of fitness for a particular purpose. No warranty may be created or extended by sales or promotional materials. The advice and strategies contained herein may not be suitable for every situation. This work is sold with the understanding that the Publisher is not engaged in rendering medical, legal, or other professional advice or services. If professional assistance is required, the services of a competent professional person should be sought. Neither the Publisher nor the author shall be liable for damages arising herefrom. The fact that an individual, organization, or website is referred to in this work as a citation and/or potential source of further information does not mean that the author or the Publisher endorses the information the individual, organization, or website may provide or recommendations they/it may make. Further, readers should be aware that Internet websites listed in this work may have changed or disappeared between when this work was written and when it is read.

For general information on our other products and services or to obtain technical support, please contact our Customer Care Department within the United States at (866) 744-2665, or outside the United States at (510) 253-0500.

Rockridge Press publishes its books in a variety of electronic and print formats. Some content that appears in print may not be available in electronic books, and vice versa.

TRADEMARKS: Rockridge Press and the Rockridge Press logo are trademarks or registered trademarks of Callisto Media Inc. and/or its affiliates, in the United States and other countries, and may not be used without written permission. All other trademarks are the property of their respective owners. Rockridge Press is not associated with any product or vendor mentioned in this book.

Interior and Cover Designer: Suzanne LaGasa
Photo Art Director: Sue Bischofberger
Editor: Susan Randol
Production Editor: Andrew Yackira
Photography: © DONOT6_STUDIO/shutterstock, p. ii; © FatCamera/iStock, p. xii; © Jacob Lund/shutterstock, p. 14; © Oksana Kuzmina/shutterstock, p. 40; © fizkes/shutterstock, p. 66; © Sasha_Litt/iStock, p. 94; © Tomsickova Tatyana/shutterstock, p. 124; © Oksana Kuzmina /shutterstock, p. 156; © Monkey Business Images/shutterstock, p. 161
Illustrations: © 2019 Natascha Rosenberg

ISBN: Print 978-1-64152-335-6 | eBook 978-1-64152-336-3

In memory of my grandmothers,
Grandma (Dorothy) Sarro and
Grandma (Priscilla) Sherman, for teaching me
the importance of hard work, humor, handiwork,
baked goods, and legacy.

To my mother, Tammy, for teaching me
the importance of caretaking, kindness,
and motherhood.

And to my daughter, Priscilla, for teaching me
the importance of creation, imagination,
and childhood.

Contents

CHAPTER 3: **Imagine That!** 41

CHAPTER 4: **Get Your Wiggles Out 67**

CHAPTER 6: **Bring the Outdoors In** 125

- 1 -
BRING THE FUN INSIDE

The toddler years, from one to three, are just a sweet, fleeting memory for me now that my kids—J.C., Priscilla, and Sawyer—are in adolescence and tweenhood. If I take a longer moment to ponder, though, I remember how those toddler times weren't only sweet and easy. It's in a toddler's nature to be curiously exploring, constantly testing limits, and simply touching something *all the time*. My kids were not spared those charmingly challenging toddler traits.

Getting outside to run and play is a great solution . . . if the weather is cooperating. When it's pouring, or freezing, or the temperature rises so high that your sweat seems to be sweating (my personal favorite), or you're just too tired to chase a toddler in the vastness of the outdoors, it's time for some indoor play. Use these activities to break up monotony, inspire learning and development, add some creativity to your day, and bring the fun inside!

My Toddler-Parenting Adventure

When my first son, Sawyer, was approaching his first birthday, his father's career required us to relocate. So, one summer Saturday, shortly after resigning from my art teaching position, our little family moved from our comfortable three-bedroom home neighboring my parents' farm to a tiny two-bedroom apartment in a city over four hours away. And I went swiftly from an on-the-go working mom to a stay-at-home mom in an area where I knew no one.

Partially to ease the jarring transition, but also because my young son needed and demanded it, I threw myself wholly into my sole job—being his mom. Every new skill and curiosity of my little guy captivated me.

While embracing my new nonprofessional life, I found myself dipping into my professional background, like the knowledge acquired in grad school child development classes or while trying to inspire creativity in rowdy middle- and high-schoolers. I discovered quickly that just a little bit of outside-the-box thinking and *a whole lot of play* made our days inside our little apartment easier, more enjoyable, and incredibly beneficial for my toddler's development.

Ironically, that play and learning with my toddler helped me reconnect with the professional, intellectual, and creative parts of myself, too. As a creative outlet and a way to connect with other moms, I began sharing our activities on a blog, B-InspiredMama.com. Throughout the past 10 years and the addition of two more incredible, creative kids, B-Inspired Mama has grown to include thousands of ideas for arts and crafts, learning activities, kid-friendly recipes, and creative parenting.

The Power of Play

The National Association for the Education of Young Children (NAEYC) makes a compelling argument for the importance of play in an article in their journal *Young Children*.

"Monkeys play. Dogs play. Rats play. Even octopuses play. And without any instruction, children of all races and genders, in all cultures of the world, invent and reinvent play in every generation. Something this ubiquitous must provide evolutionary advantages to both animals and humans. Decades of research suggest just that."

They go on to outline research and case studies showcasing the benefits of free play and guided play to create "playful learning." One of those studies identifies four key ingredients that make up successful learning: the child is a "mentally active" participant, the child is "engaged" without distraction, the play is "socially interactive" with peers and adults, and last, but certainly not least, the play includes a "meaningful connection" to the child's life.

Play is incredibly beneficial for your child's learning and development, and your role in that play is powerful. This book makes incorporating the elements of successful learning both easy and fun, no matter the weather.

Toddler Time

Maybe it's because my kids are nearing their tween and teen years *(please pray for me!)*, but the toddler years are the parenting years I miss the most. Toddlers are like little balls of curious energy bursting open with new skills and learning every day. It's an exciting time for them and for us!

Before we look at the skills they're developing, let me share a quick word of warning from a fellow mama who's been there: Don't let all these developmental milestones worry you so much that it hinders your relationship and connection with your child. I know you hear it all the time, but I've seen it with my kids firsthand: Every child develops at their own pace and in their own way. So, monitor your child's development with the guidance of your pediatrician and consider the milestones on the following pages when choosing developmentally appropriate activities for your child, but follow your child's lead and your mama instincts, too.

12 to 18 Months

Rapid physical growth throughout infancy starts to slow as babies reach their first birthday and move into toddlerhood. The focus shifts to how their bodies move in space and interact with the world around them while they work on mastering new skills. Here are some specific skills that start emerging:

Gross Motor Skills

- Stands without support
- Walks with few falls
- Squats to pick something up
- Sits independently on a chair
- Climbs stairs or furniture
- Tosses a ball underhand while seated

Fine Motor Skills

- Claps their hands
- Waves goodbye
- Holds a crayon and scribbles
- Uses fingertips to pick up small objects
- Drinks from a cup
- Uses a spoon
- Scoops materials for play
- Stacks a few objects
- Bangs objects together

Language & Social-Emotional Development

- Continues babbling
- May use five to ten words
- Points at familiar people and objects in pictures
- Imitates others during play
- Can identify a few body parts
- Nods or shakes head to respond to yes/no questions
- Follows simple directions
- Has an interest in interacting with people
- Can locate objects when pointed to
- Turns head in response to hearing their name

18 to 24 Months

As toddlers approach their second birthday, social and play skills expand. While they still primarily imitate during play, they start to interact more with others and even delve into some pretend play, too. Here are some specific skills they often exhibit:

Gross Motor Skills

- Walks and runs
- Coordinates movements for play
- Jumps with feet together
- Walks up and down stairs
- Throws a ball into a box
- Uses ride-on toys

Fine Motor Skills

- Uses fingers and thumbs to hold crayons
- Opens containers
- Turns the pages of a book
- Scribble-writes with writing tools
- Builds with four or more blocks
- Turns over and pours out containers

Language & Social-Emotional Skills

- Starts to use two-word phrases
- Can name objects in pictures
- Understands action words
- Starts to use pronouns (you, my, me)
- Can identify three to five body parts
- Follows simple two-step directions
- Turns head when they hear their name
- Interacts with others during play
- May play with toys without mouthing them
- Enjoys directing play

24 to 36 Months

After toddlers turn two years old, their cognitive, language, and social-emotional learning take center stage over the previous year's focus on physical development. Their social-emotional growth brings along a desire for more independence as well. That—combined with expanding language skills helping them communicate their wants (and their "NO!"s)—can prove to be quite challenging. Here are the important skills they're developing:

Gross Motor Skills

- Kicks a ball forward
- Can stand on tiptoes
- Pulls toys behind while walking
- Carries large toys while walking
- Can ride a tricycle
- Catches a large ball
- Jumps over an object
- Walks along a balance beam

Fine Motor Skills

- Uses a pincer grasp to pick up small objects
- Turns door handles
- Screws lid on a container
- Can string large beads
- Starts to draw squares and circles

Language & Social-Emotional Skills

- Uses two- to four-word sentences
- Talks understandably
- Demonstrates increasing independence
- Plays make-believe
- Begins to sort objects by colors and shapes
- Starts to understand "same" and "different"
- Enjoys listening to and telling stories
- Starts to count and understand numbers
- Becomes increasingly inventive during play

Each indoor play activity in this book includes simple icons indicating the developmental skills and learning concepts that activity reinforces. However, because play has such inherent developmental and educational benefits, most activities actually strengthen far more skills than the icons indicate. Use the icons to choose activities if you're looking to work on specific skills or concepts with your toddler, but remember, you can't go wrong by following your child's curiosity and harnessing the natural benefits of play.

Skills Learned

colors

listening

problem-solving

creativity

memory

science

early literacy

mindfulness

sensory development

fine motor skills

1 2 3
numbers and counting

shapes and letters

gross motor skills

oral motor
development

social-emotional
development

imagination

patterns

sorting

language development

visual spatial skills

Safety First!

You'll notice some activities have a note of **Caution!** I tried to remember all of the wild predicaments my toddlers got in years ago—as well as anticipate other potential scenarios—to make each specific activity as safe as possible. However, be sure to follow these general safety guidelines when doing *any* of the play activities with your toddler.

- Consider your toddler's development and abilities when choosing activities. Monitor and assist, as needed, when trying advanced activities.

- Avoid activities with small materials if your toddler mouths objects during play.

- *Always* supervise closely during water play and never leave bins or bathtubs of water unattended.

- Keep your toddler away from sharp scissors, knives, hot glue guns, and other potentially hazardous tools. If possible, perform any prep requiring these tools when your toddler is napping or not present.

- Whenever possible, choose nontoxic, kid-friendly art supplies and materials. If a material is new to you and likely to come in contact with your toddler's skin, test it on a small area before play.

- Some play materials and setups could pose tripping, slipping, falling, choking, and strangulation hazards if left unsupervised. Take down and put away all play setups after play has ended.

- All of the activities are designed for your toddler and you. Always supervise during play.

How to Use This Book

My hope for this book of over 100 rainy day toddler activities, as was my hope with my previous book of outdoor play activities, is that it makes it *easier* for you to incorporate more intentional play, meaningful connection, playful learning, and fun into your days with your toddler. Here are some tips for using this book to increase the indoor fun:

Being inside doesn't have to mean less fun! The activities have been sorted into five categories that are perfectly suited to a toddler's natural curiosity and high energy. These activities will inspire creativity, encourage imagination, harness toddler energy, encourage focused learning, and explore nature and the world in your home. You'll find the perfect activity for any indoor scenario, toddler interest, or materials and toys you already have around the house.

Use what you have. Hard-to-find materials, potentially dangerous tools, and complicated prep just don't mix with toddlerhood. The activities in this book use simple materials and offer substitutions whenever possible. Some use basic craft supplies, like pom-poms, construction paper, or washable markers. Others take advantage of household items, like plastic food storage containers, cotton balls, or the laundry basket. And a few require no materials at all!

Keep the essentials handy. A few everyday items are used over and over throughout this book. I suggest you purchase some exclusively for play so they're always ready to go and easy to locate, and you don't have to stress over them getting messy. Make a simple activity kit inside a large plastic bin or laundry basket that includes different sizes of food storage containers and shallow plastic bins, a large divided plastic tray, a baking sheet, a muffin pan or two, different types of scoops, sets of measuring cups and spoons, a roll of aluminum foil, some zip-top bags, disposable dishware left over from parties, and old sheets, blankets, or disposable plastic party tablecloths for covering surfaces. Add to it over time as you find affordable items at thrift stores, dollar stores, and yard sales.

Think outside the same old spot. Don't get stuck thinking your toddler should only do activities while sitting at the dining room table. Toddlers often work well (and get great sensory and motor skill benefits) by working on vertical surfaces or on the floor. Consider every location in the house when planning indoor activities. Maybe the kitchen floor is the easiest to clean, making it perfect for foamy sensory play. Or maybe the bathtub keeps your little one happy in one spot long enough to engage in an alphabet game. Don't limit yourself to where you think activities *should* be done. Do what works for you, your toddler, and your home.

Prep when you can. The activities have been designed to get the most benefit possible with the least amount of prep possible. When prep is included, it's to make it easier for you, safer for your toddler, or to aid the learning or developmental benefits. Sometimes you can even include your toddler in prep, depending on her temperament, developmental level, and the materials involved. Each activity includes the time estimate for prep, with many requiring no prep at all, some requiring up to five minutes, and just a few that take a bit longer.

Consider your toddler's attention span and your time. Each activity includes a time estimate, though all activities are suited to a toddler's short attention span, rarely lasting more than 20 minutes. Use the time estimates to choose the right activities for your toddler's attention span and temperament-of-the-moment. Never feel obligated to fully complete activities after your toddler loses interest.

Let the activities inspire you, not limit you! The material lists, prep, and steps are meant to make things easy for you, but don't let them limit you. Always feel free to try similar materials that you already have. Experiment with different ways of doing something. Go wild and use letters instead of numbers! All kidding aside, let these activities be a jumping-off point for you and your toddler, not a constraint.

When all else fails, follow your toddler's lead. The activities are heavily focused on learning and strengthening development with natural integration of fine motor skill practice, gross motor movements, sounds and singing, colors, numbers, and the ABCs. But remember, your toddler knows how to learn through play already. Never force skills or learning on a toddler who isn't interested or ready. Always follow your toddler's lead.

Don't try to do it all. While I would be flattered, I wouldn't expect a toddler parent or caregiver to have time to read this entire book in one sitting, or even at all! Instead, grab it during naptime to find an active game in chapter 4 for when your toddler wakes up ready to run. Keep it handy to pick an activity from chapter 5 when you need some calm-down time. Or spend 10 minutes in bed finding and marking some fun activities for the next day. And don't ever think you should or could do it all.

Every little bit counts! Nope, you can't do it all. But you can do something. And every little bit of something—of play and connection with your toddler—counts immensely. Those singular moments will roll and grow like a giant snowball to be far greater and more sparkly and beautiful than you could ever have imagined.

More friends equal more fun. If your toddler has siblings, cousins, or friends around, try a group activity. In each chapter, look for the "Rainy Day Fun Together" sidebar. From a spirited indoor relay race to a silly animal sound symphony, these activities are fun for all ages and group sizes.

Ultimately, don't let being indoors hamper the fun. Instead, use these activities to entertain your toddler, encourage a little learning and creativity, and make some meaningful memories.

- 2 -
CRAFTY CREATIONS

Yes, toddler arts and crafts often include mess. It's definitely tempting to just skip them, considering the many messes your toddler likely already makes throughout the day. But arts and crafts activities provide incredible opportunities for diverse sensory experiences, fine motor skill practice, problem-solving, and creative exploration. Plus, you get to engage with your toddler and pass the time in a fun, creative way on those long days indoors. But, actually, toddler arts and crafts don't have to be horribly messy. Carefully chosen supplies, clear simple steps, and helpful tips in the creative activities ahead will ensure your arts and crafts time is indoor friendly and toddler approved.

Wild Hair, Don't Care!

Pipe cleaner hair that your child can style makes this craft a toddler hit. Plus, it's a fun way to sneak in some fine motor skill practice.

Messiness: 1
Prep Time: **None**
Activity Time: **20 minutes**

MATERIALS

Double-sided tape

Cardboard tube

10 to 12 pipe cleaners

Decorative craft tape, or painter's tape

Washable markers

Self-adhesive googly eyes

Stickers

Yarn (optional)

Safety scissors (optional)

STEPS

1. Wrap a piece of double-sided tape around one end of the cardboard tube. Help your child press a half inch of one end of the pipe cleaners onto the sticky tape around the tube, leaving a little space between each one. Wrap decorative tape around the pipe cleaner ends on the tube, pressing it in between them to secure them well.

2. Have your toddler bring his tube person to life by using washable markers and self-adhesive googly eyes to add a face.

3. Allow him to be creative in decorating the rest of the tube with markers and stickers.

4. Encourage him to bend and style his tube person's wild pipe cleaner hair.

TIP *Try making another tube person with yarn hair so your child can give it a haircut and practice scissor skills.*

CAUTION! *Skip the googly eyes if your child often puts objects in his mouth during play. Draw the eyes on with marker instead.*

SKILLS
LEARNED

creativity

fine
motor skills

sensory
development

social-emotional
development

Fingerprints on the Heart Keepsakes

Preserve your little one's tiny fingerprints with a sensory-rich ornament craft. The finished ornaments make a sweet gift for grandparents, caregivers, or teachers, too.

Messiness: 4
Prep Time: None
Activity Time: 20 minutes + drying time

MATERIALS

Cornstarch

Air-dry clay (recipe on page 19 or store-bought)

Rolling pin (optional)

Heart cookie cutter

Small spatula or spreader

Baking sheet, lined with wax paper

Straw

Ribbon, 1 (6-inch) length per ornament

Acrylic paint, paintbrush, fine point permanent marker, and waterbase sealer (optional)

STEPS

1. On a cornstarch-dusted surface, help your child flatten the clay until it's about a half-inch thick. Use a rolling pin, if possible.

2. Have him use the cookie cutter to cut hearts out of the clay and use a spatula to help him transfer the hearts onto the wax paper–lined baking sheet.

3. Help him lightly press fingerprint polka dots into the hearts.

4. Use a straw to poke a hole in the top of each heart, and leave them to dry overnight, or until fully dry and hardened.

5. Tie a loop of ribbon through the hole in each ornament for hanging.

TIP *If you're gifting the ornaments, you can fancy them up by using acrylic paint to color the inside of the fingerprint or allow your child to paint all over them. After the paint dries, use a permanent marker to write: "Your fingerprints will never fade from my heart!" along with the current year and your child's name on the backs. Seal them with waterbase sealer for durability.*

Air-Dry Clay Recipe

MATERIALS

Measuring cups

1 bottle
(about 5 to 6 ounces)
white glue

Mixing bowl

1 to 1½ cups
cornstarch

Add the glue to a mixing bowl. Add in small amounts of cornstarch at a time, stirring with a wooden spoon thoroughly until the mixture forms a dough. Have your toddler knead the dough on a cornstarch-dusted surface until it reaches a workable nonsticky dough consistency. Knead in more cornstarch or glue, as needed.

Abstract Bath Art

Use just one popular kids' craft material to add some creative shape learning to your toddler's day—right in the bathtub.

Messiness: 1
Prep Time: 5 minutes
Activity Time: 15 minutes

MATERIALS

Craft foam sheets, in various colors

Scissors

Gallon-size plastic zip-top bag

TIP *Full sheets and precut shapes of craft foam can be found in the craft sections of most stores. Cutting unique shapes works best, but precut shapes would also work.*

PREP

Cut multiple triangles, rectangles, squares, and circles of various sizes out of the foam sheets. Store them in a zip-top bag in the bathroom so they are handy during bath time.

STEPS

1. Fill the bathtub with water and help your little one into it. Dump the foam shapes out of the bag and into the water.

2. Allow her to explore the floating shapes. Help her identify the shapes and colors.

3. Show her how the water helps the shapes stick to the bathroom wall and side of the tub. Encourage her to stick them on the wall in different designs and patterns. If they don't stick well, make floating designs on the water instead. Explain that she is making abstract art, saying something like, "Abstract art has only shapes, colors, and lines; no recognizable things or people."

4. Challenge her further to identify the colors and shapes in her abstract bath art.

CAUTION! *Keep your toddler away from sharp scissors. Always supervise your toddler closely around water.*

"See the Sparkle" Eyeglasses

Tell your toddler these homemade eyeglasses are magic, helping her only see the "sparkle," or good parts of people and the world around her.

Messiness: 1
Prep Time: None
Activity Time: 15 minutes

MATERIALS

2 (6- to 12-ounce) white paper cups

Scissors

Self-adhesive gems, or small shiny stickers

Sparkly pipe cleaners

STEPS

1. Cut across each cup about a half inch up from the bottom. Cut a circle out of each cup's bottom, turning them into rings that will become the eyeglass frames.

2. Allow your toddler to decorate the ring eyeglass frames with gems.

3. Help her twist a pipe cleaner onto the rings as a nosepiece to connect them. Twist a longer pipe cleaner on each of the opposite sides of the rings for bending around the ears to hold the eyeglasses on. Trim the pipe cleaners with scissors, as needed.

4. Help your toddler put on her "See the Sparkle" eyeglasses and discuss the importance of focusing on the good in people and the world around her.

CAUTION! *Skip the small gems if your toddler is likely to put them in her mouth. Always keep your child away from sharp scissors.*

SKILLS
LEARNED

science

sensory
development

visual
spatial skills

Footprint Fossil Matching Game

Help your toddler make his own fossils using his plastic dinosaur or animal toys. Then use your homemade fossils for a fun and educational matching game.

Messiness: **4**
Prep Time: **None**
Activity Time: **20 minutes +
drying time**

MATERIALS

Air-dry clay
(recipe on page 19 or
store-bought)

Baking sheet, lined
with wax paper

Water-friendly
plastic dinosaur
or animal toys

Medium plastic bin
(optional)

Water and kid-friendly
liquid soap (optional)

STEPS

1. Help your child roll a handful of clay into a ball and place it on a wax paper-lined baking sheet. Flatten the ball.

2. Have him choose a dinosaur toy and press its foot into the clay to create a footprint.

3. Repeat, having him use a different dinosaur for each ball of clay. Leave the fossils on the pan overnight to dry.

4. Use the hardened footprint fossils and the dinosaur toys to play a simple foot-to-footprint fossil matching game. Allow the fossils to inspire imaginative play, too.

TIP *Add to the fun (and sensory experience) by allowing your little one to give the toys a bath in a bin of soapy water after fossil making.*

Stamp a Fruit & Veggie Apron

Incorporate some science into your toddler's day by inspecting the insides of cut fruits and vegetables and discovering the prints each one makes when it is used as a stamp.

Messiness: 4
Prep Time: 10 minutes
Activity Time: 20 minutes + drying time

MATERIALS

Black acrylic paint

Large divided plastic tray, or 2 large plastic plates

Fruits and vegetables, such as apple, orange, celery, artichoke, bell pepper, okra, and onion

Paring knife

Paper towels

Large sheet of cardboard, or newspaper

White apron, or large white paper

PREP

1. Add a thin layer of paint to one section of the divided tray.

2. Cut each fruit and vegetable so its cut edge can be used for stamping. Place them in the remaining sections on the tray. Add some paper towels under juicy ones to absorb the liquid.

3. Place the cardboard on the floor or table and spread the apron out on it.

STEPS

1. Invite your child to examine each cut piece of fruit and vegetable. Help her identify each and inspect the insides and any seeds.

2. Have her choose one and help her dip the cut side into paint and then stamp it onto the apron.

3. Repeat, allowing her to stamp the different fruits and vegetables randomly all over the apron.

4. Leave the apron flat until dry. Then put it in a hot dryer for 30 minutes to set the paint.

TIP *No apron? Stamp on a piece of large white paper or cardboard instead.*

CAUTION! *Keep your toddler away from sharp knives.*

Drippy-Color-Mixy Garland

Invite your toddler to experience the inspirational magic of mixing colors. Then, after it's dry, make a simple garland with his colorful art.

Messiness: 3
Prep Time: None
Activity Time: 20 minutes + drying time

MATERIALS

3 basket-style drip coffee maker filters

2 baking sheets, or plastic trays

Washable markers

Medicine dropper

Small bowl of water

Glue stick

String

STEPS

1. Spread the coffee filters out on the baking sheets and have your toddler help flatten them.

2. Allow him to color the coffee filters with the washable markers, covering them as much as possible with multiple colors.

3. Show him how to fill the medicine dropper with water from the bowl and drip drops of water all over the coffee filters. Notice and discuss the effects the water has on the markers and colors. Leave them on the trays until fully dry.

4. To make the garland, fold each dry coffee filter in half to crease it. Open them and lay them in a row with the creases lined up. Apply glue along the creases. Place the string across the glue, leaving extra string on each end for hanging. Fold each coffee filter in half at the crease, sandwiching the string inside. Hang your colorful garland in a sunny window.

CAUTION! *When hanging the garland, make sure it is secure from falling and high enough to be out of reach of your toddler.*

Emotion Spoon Puppets

These simple spoon puppets will inspire lots of imaginative fun, plus some valuable social-emotional learning, too.

Messiness: 2
Prep Time: None
Activity Time: 10 minutes

MATERIALS

3 to 5 wooden spoons

Decorative craft tape

Small stickers

Self-adhesive googly eyes

Black permanent marker

STEPS

1. Allow your toddler to decorate the handles of each spoon with small pieces of tape and stickers. Help her rip off small pieces of tape, as needed.

2. Have her apply two googly eyes on each spoon's bowl. Use the permanent marker to draw a mouth on each, representing different emotions, such as a sad frown, a happy toothy smile, an angry slant-line mouth, or a surprised oval mouth.

3. Use your new puppets to act out scenes and discuss emotions with your child.

CAUTION! *Skip the googly eyes if your child often puts objects in her mouth. Draw the eyes on instead.*

Bendy-Leg Bugs

Get ready for an infestation of cuteness when you realize how fun and easy these bendy-leg bugs are to make with your toddler.

Messiness: 2
Prep Time: None
Activity Time: 15 minutes

MATERIALS

Crayons

Wooden craft sticks

Pipe cleaners

Self-adhesive googly eyes

Pictures of insects, in a book or online (optional)

Marker (optional)

STEPS

1. Have your child use crayons to draw stripes along the craft sticks. Add some simple pattern learning by showing him how to draw stripes in an AB pattern (*red, orange, red, orange...*) or an AAB pattern (*red, red, orange, red, red, orange...*).

2. Help him add bendy legs by wrapping and twisting pipe cleaners along the stick.

3. Add googly eyes, then encourage your child to play imaginatively with his bendy-leg bug.

TIP *Add some science learning by looking at pictures of insects beforehand and discussing their characteristics and number of legs.*

CAUTION! *Skip the googly eyes if your child often puts objects in his mouth and draw the eyes on with marker instead. Fold any sharp pipe cleaner ends over.*

From White to Black Collage

This collage craft offers an opportunity for your toddler to explore various textures and basic shapes, all in shades of gray from black to white.

Messiness: **4**
Prep Time: **5 minutes**
Activity Time: **10 minutes**

MATERIALS

Newspaper

Materials of various textures and shades of black, gray, and white, such as newspaper, cotton balls, dry rice, dry black beans, cotton swabs, Bubble Wrap, or aluminum foil

Scissors

Large divided plastic tray

Paintbrush

Small container of white glue

Shoebox lid, or other shallow cardboard box

PREP

1. Cover your crafting surface with newspaper; this one gets sticky!

2. Cut any large textured materials (such as newspaper, Bubble Wrap, or foil) into basic shapes. Arrange the textured materials in a divided tray.

STEPS

1. Invite your child to examine the different textures of the materials. Encourage her to describe what her fingers are feeling using words like *soft, bumpy, rough,* and *smooth.*

2. Assist your toddler in painting glue inside the box lid and adhering various textured materials to it. Encourage her to identify the shapes of the materials.

3. Explain that she is making a collage, which is "art made by sticking down lots of different things." Leave it flat to dry.

CAUTION! *Skip small materials if your child often puts objects in her mouth. Always keep your child away from sharp scissors.*

Bead Pattern Bowl

This simple craft offers lots of fine-motor-skill and pincer-grasp practice. Plus, you can teach your toddler about simple patterns.

Messiness: **4**
Prep Time: **None**
Activity Time: **20 minutes +** drying time

MATERIALS

Plastic wrap

Air-dry clay
(recipe on page 19 or store-bought)

Rolling pin (optional)

Small or medium plastic bowl

Beads, various sizes and colors

STEPS

1. On a plastic wrap–covered surface, help your child flatten the clay to about a half inch in thickness. Use a rolling pin, if possible.

2. Use the plastic wrap to carefully lift and transfer the flattened clay into the bowl. Allow your toddler to help smooth it on the bottom and inside sides of the bowl and remove any clay hanging over the edges.

3. Invite your toddler to press beads into the clay. Show him how to place beads side by side to make lines and use those lines to make shapes and designs.

4. Challenge him by having him try placing beads in a simple AB pattern (*red, orange, red, orange…*) or an AAB pattern (*red, red, orange, red, red, orange…*).

5. Leave to dry overnight, or until fully hardened, before removing it from the bowl and peeling the plastic off the bottom.

CAUTION! *This activity may not be suitable for children who put objects in their mouths during play.*

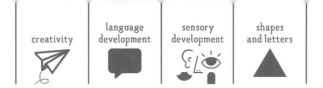
Texture & Shape Block Stamps

Stamping is a very toddler-friendly art activity. Make your own block stamps for your child to explore textures and shapes.

Messiness: 4
Prep Time: None
Activity Time: 20 minutes

MATERIALS

6 wooden toy blocks

6 different textured materials, such as Bubble Wrap, mesh produce bag, aluminum foil, a doily, or corrugated cardboard

Rubber bands

Scissors (optional)

Foam shape stickers

Washable paint, black

Large plastic tray

Construction paper

STEPS

1. Together with your child, turn each block into a stamp.

2. Wrap the first block in a textured material, using rubber bands to hold it on. You can cut the material to be easier to manage if you'd like.

3. Apply foam shape stickers to one side of a block. Wrap a bunch of rubber bands around a block. Repeat this until all the blocks are covered and can be used as a stamp.

4. Place the block stamps on one side of the tray and some paint on the other.

5. Have her choose a block stamp, identify and discuss its shape and texture, then dip the textured side in the paint and stamp it on the paper.

6. Repeat, stamping each block randomly on the paper.

TIP *Try stamping blocks that already have textured or raised surfaces, too.*

CAUTION! *Skip small foam stickers if your child is likely to put them in her mouth. Always keep your child away from sharp scissors.*

SKILLS
LEARNED   colors   creativity   fine   sensory
                                         motor skills   development

Sticky Stained Glass Window

Sticky contact paper makes this toddler art activity easy and low mess.

Messiness: 2
Prep Time: 5 minutes
Activity Time: 20 minutes

MATERIALS

Tape

Clear contact paper

Black yarn, in various short lengths

Tissue paper squares, in various colors

PREP

Tape a large rectangle of contact paper, sticky side facing you, onto a window within your child's reach.

STEPS

1. Encourage your child to make lines on the contact paper by sticking on pieces of yarn.

2. Have him fill the sticky spaces around the lines with tissue paper.

3. Help him identify the colors and notice the sunlight shining through, like a stained glass window.

4. Want to keep it afterward? Remove it from the window and place another piece of clear sticky contact paper on it to sandwich the yarn and paper art inside.

SKILLS
LEARNED   creativity   fine
motor skills   science

Magical Starry Sky

Your toddler will think it's magical to see the stars appear as she paints!

Messiness: 2
Prep Time: 5 minutes
Activity Time: 10 minutes

MATERIALS

White crayon

Watercolor paper,
or other heavyweight
paper

Paintbrush

Watercolor paints

Paper towels

Small container
with water

PREP

Without your toddler seeing, use the white
crayon to draw various stars, clouds, and swirls
on the watercolor paper.

STEPS

1. Invite your toddler to paint the paper with the
   paintbrush and watercolor paints. Help her use
   paper towels and a small container of water to
   clean the brush between colors.

2. Encourage her to use different colors and watch
   colors spread and mix.

3. Watch her excitement when the stars, clouds, and
   swirls magically appear.

4. Explain the "magic" science of the white crayon
   wax resisting the watercolor paint and allow her
   to experiment on another piece of paper with
   the crayon and watercolor paints.

TIP *Add some art history learning by showing your
child Vincent van Gogh's famous painting* Starry
Night. *Find it online or at the library.*

Collaborative Canister Sculpture

This group art activity invites each child to design their own parts for a larger collaborative sculpture.

Messiness: 2
Prep Time: None
Activity Time: 20 minutes

MATERIALS

2 (or more) empty canisters with lids per child, such as containers from rolled oats, hot chocolate, or potato chips

White paper

Tape

Decorative craft tape, or colored electrical tape

Stickers (optional)

Washable markers (optional)

STEPS

1. Together, wrap each canister with white paper, using tape, as needed.

2. Have each child choose a different color and use that color of tape, stickers, and/or washable markers to decorate their canisters.

3. Challenge the kids to work together to stack and arrange the canisters into one large sculpture.

SKILLS
LEARNED

colors

gross
motor skills

visual
spatial skills

Color Spy Assemblage

This easy activity invites your toddler on a color hunt around the house to find objects for a color-themed assemblage.

Messiness: 2
Prep Time: None
Activity Time: 20 minutes

MATERIALS

Toys and household objects around the house

Basket

White poster board, or large white paper

STEPS

1. Have your toddler choose a color, then hunt around the house for small toys or objects of that color. Use a basket to collect them, or burn some energy finding one at a time.

2. Place the poster board on the floor and arrange the objects on it, leaving just a small space between each object to make an assemblage. Explain by saying something like, "An assemblage is art made by grouping many objects together."

3. Play a game of "I Spy" by taking turns calling out an object you see in the assemblage for the other person to find and point to. Then, have your child help put the objects away.

TIP *Want to preserve your color assemblage? Photograph it from above, then print the photo to play future "I Spy" games with. Do this each time you make a different color assemblage and add the photos to a mini album to make your own color spy book.*

Shiny Robot Sculpture

You've got all the materials you need right in the recycling bin to inspire some creative robot sculpture making.

Messiness: 3
Prep Time: None
Activity Time: 20 minutes

MATERIALS

Various objects from the recycling bin, like plastic bottles, egg cartons, jar lids, cardboard tubes, milk cartons, or small boxes

Tape, various types

Scissors

Aluminum foil

Sparkly pipe cleaners

Craft glue (optional)

STEPS

1. Examine the recycled objects together, brain-storming the robot parts each one could be.

2. Help your child combine the objects to create a robot sculpture. Use tape and scissors as needed.

3. Wrap the robot sculpture or certain parts of it in aluminum foil, using tape, as needed.

4. Poke holes to attach sparkly pipe cleaners. Wind pipe cleaners around your finger to make spring-like details. Use glue, if needed, to attach the springs.

CAUTION! *Do not use metal recycled materials, as they may have sharp edges. Skip small objects and bottle lids if your child is likely to put them in her mouth. Keep your child away from sharp scissors.*

Shape Castle Collage

Invite your toddler to explore triangles, squares, and rectangles with this castle-themed art project.

Messiness: 2
Prep Time: 5 minutes
Activity Time: 10 minutes

MATERIALS

Construction paper, in various colors

Scissors

Tray

Large black paper

Glue stick

Black washable marker

PREP

Cut construction paper into rectangles, squares, and triangles of various sizes and colors.

STEPS

1. Present the paper shapes, all mixed together, on a tray. Challenge your toddler by having him identify the shapes and colors while sorting by shape.

2. Offer a large piece of black paper, and have him glue shapes onto it, overlapping and layering as desired, to create a castle. Encourage more shape and color recognition while doing so.

3. Use the washable marker to add details (like windowpanes or stones) to the shape castle.

CAUTION! *Always keep your child away from sharp scissors.*

Finger Paint Color-Mixing Monoprints

Finger painting might be a bit messy, but it's so fun and beneficial for little fingers!

Messiness: 5
Prep Time: None
Activity Time: 10 minutes

MATERIALS

Washable finger paint, in primary colors: red, yellow, and blue

Baking sheet

Heavyweight paper

STEPS

1. Add the paint colors to the baking sheet. Allow your child to explore the paint with her fingers.

2. Share in her excitement when she sees the colors mix and make a new color.

3. Have her smooth the paint, then draw lines in it with her finger. Encourage her to try making different types of lines, like wavy, zigzag, dashed, and curvy.

4. Press a piece of paper onto the paint, then lift it to see the monoprint on the paper. Set aside to dry. Repeat, adding more paint, as needed.

TIP *Have your child practice writing letters and numbers in the paint, then monoprinting them.*

SKILLS
LEARNED

creativity

fine
motor skills

patterns

Cookie-Cutter Table Runner

Cookie-cutter painting was a go-to art project when my kids were little. It's perfect for large-scale art, like this painted table runner.

Messiness: 4
Prep Time: 5 minutes
Activity Time: 15 minutes

MATERIALS

Painter's tape, or other tape

Roll paper, or the back of wrapping paper

Washable paints

Paper plates

Cookie cutters

PREP

1. Tape a long length of paper onto a hard floor or table.

2. Squirt each color of paint on its own plate. Place a cookie cutter on each.

STEPS

1. Demonstrate how to dip a cookie cutter in paint and stamp it on the paper. Invite your child to stamp the paper with the various cookie cutters. Keep each cookie cutter with its own paint.

2. Add some learning by challenging your toddler to stamp the cookie cutters in simple patterns along the paper.

3. After the paint dries, use the paper as a table runner.

   TIP *Use holiday or seasonal cookie cutters to create a table runner for a holiday party.*

Bathtub Spray Art

This open-ended art activity allows for easy cleanup; it's done right in the bathtub!

Messiness: 2
Prep Time: None
Activity Time: 15 minutes

MATERIALS

Watercolor paper, or other heavyweight paper

Washable markers

Spray bottle

Water

STEPS

1. Have your child draw on the paper with the washable markers. Allow her to draw or scribble any way she wants.

2. Place her art inside the bottom of the bathtub. Then invite her to sit outside the tub and spray water on her marker art using the spray bottle.

3. Discuss how the water causes the marker to spread and mix. Encourage lots of color-recognition practice.

TIP *To add some learning, draw shapes, numbers, or letters on the paper. Then call them out for your child to find and spray.*

CAUTION! *Test your markers on the bathtub before play if you're worried about staining.*

- 3 -
IMAGINE THAT!

Considering my background in art education, one might assume that my favorite aspect of parenting would be arts and crafts. I do love a kids' art project, but my favorite part of toddler parenting was actually observing their unfolding imaginations!

Imaginative play, pretend play, make-believe, whatever name you give it, is essential for early childhood development. Young toddlers are often preoccupied with simply exploring the world, perfecting new skills, and interacting with their environment and objects in very literal ways. But as toddlers master those skills, their thinking takes a more symbolic and imaginative turn. They start to understand that words have meanings, pictures and books tell stories, and they can be any person with any profession anytime they want!

The upcoming activities will nurture your toddler's budding complex symbolic thinking and inspire further social-emotional learning through imaginative play.

Scoops & Sundaes

Not only is this pretend ice cream play fun and imaginative, but the ice cream scooping offers lots of coordination and motor skill practice, too.

Messiness: 2
Prep Time: **None**
Activity Time: 20 minutes

MATERIALS

Construction paper, in "ice cream" colors like white, brown, and pink

Empty ice cream cartons, clean and dry

Plastic bowls and spoons

Ice cream scoop

Ice cream cones, or cones made with paper (optional)

Cotton balls

Red pom-poms

Sequins

STEPS

1. Have your child make scoops of ice cream by crumpling construction paper into balls. Place them into the ice cream cartons.

2. Invite her to play ice cream shop using the paper ice cream, real bowls, spoons, an ice cream scoop, and cones (if possible). Cotton balls make great pretend whipped cream, red pom-poms are excellent cherries, and sequins are perfect as sprinkles.

3. Encourage listening, memory, and early math skills by ordering ice cream cones and sundaes with specific scoops and toppings.

CAUTION! *Skip the pom-poms and sequins if your child often puts objects in her mouth.*

Phone Number Song Fun

Make a pretend smartphone and use it, along with this clever song, to teach your toddler your phone number.

Messiness: 2
Prep Time: **None**
Activity Time: **15 minutes**

MATERIALS

Markers

Cardboard, about 3 x 5 inches

Picture of parent (optional)

Glue stick (optional)

STEPS

1. Using the markers, draw small circle phone buttons on the bottom half of the cardboard. Write the numbers 1 through 9, then *, 0, and #, inside the circles.

2. If you have a picture of the person whose phone number is being memorized, help your toddler glue it above the phone buttons.

3. Together with your child, use the pretend phone to practice learning the phone number. Encourage him to press the number buttons as he sings the phone number song to the tune of "Frère Jacques (Are You Sleeping?)."

   Example: If mom's phone number is 470-555-1234, sing:

   4-7-0, 4-7-0,

   5-5-5, 5-5-5,

   1-2-3-4, 1-2-3-4,

   That's my mom, that's my mom.

SKILLS
LEARNED

imagination

language
development

social-emotional
development

Pillowcase Puppet Theater

Use an everyday household item to transform a dining room chair into your child's very own puppet theater.

Messiness: 1
Prep Time: 10 minutes
Activity Time: 10 minutes

MATERIALS

An old pillowcase

Duct tape, in various colors and/or patterns

Black permanent marker

Dining chair

Puppets (Emotion Spoon Puppets on page 25 or store-bought)

PREP

1. Lay the pillowcase vertically, open-side down, on a flat surface.

2. Add colorful stripes of duct tape horizontally across the pillowcase.

3. Use the permanent marker to write "[Name]'s Puppet Theater" on the tape.

STEPS

1. Slide the opening of the pillowcase down over the back of a dining chair, with the decorated side on the back.

2. Invite your toddler to take turns putting on puppet shows, sitting backward on the chair and using her hand or puppets held above the pillowcase-covered chair back.

CAUTION! *Stay near your toddler while she sits backward on the chair to assist and prevent falls.*

Colorful Pasta Chef

Use up old boxes of dry pasta from your pantry for this colorful pretend play activity.

Messiness: 3
Prep Time: 10 minutes + drying time
Activity Time: 20 minutes

MATERIALS

Dry pasta of various shapes

Vinegar

Food-storage containers with tight lids, 1 per pasta shape

Food coloring, in 3 or more colors

Baking rack

Baking sheet, lined with wax paper

Large divided plastic tray, or plastic bin

Various mixing bowls, measuring cups, serving spoons, plastic dishes and utensils

PREP

1. Place some dry pasta and a teaspoon of vinegar in each container.

2. Using a different color for each container, add 10 drops of food coloring to each one, then tightly secure the lids.

3. Have your child help shake each container until the color disperses. Add more vinegar and/or food coloring, as needed.

4. Pour the pasta from each container onto a baking rack positioned over a wax paper–lined baking sheet. Allow the pasta to dry fully.

STEPS

1. Offer your toddler the colorful pasta on a divided tray, as well as the mixing bowls, measuring cups, and serving spoons.

2. Allow free play time for him to scoop, measure, pour, stir, and serve the pasta.

3. Increase the color learning by ordering specific colors of pasta and having him sort the pasta by color back into the divided tray after play.

TIP *No time to dye pasta? No worries! Your toddler can still practice scooping and pouring while playing with dry pasta right out of the box.*

CAUTION! *Avoid small pasta if your toddler is likely to put it in his mouth during play.*

Postcard Delivery

Mail delivery play with postcards provides your toddler with valuable practice in fine motor skills, early literacy, and social-emotional learning.

Messiness: 1
Prep Time: 10 minutes
Activity Time: 20 minutes

MATERIALS

File folders, or folded paper

Scissors

Tape

Markers

Postcards, both previously mailed and new, or old greeting cards

Stickers, ideally square or rectangular

TIP *Save up old greeting cards and cut the fronts off to use as pretend postcards.*

PREP

1. Make a pocket mailbox out of a file folder by cutting a couple inches off the side of the front flap and taping the other edges together.

2. Using a marker, write "[Name]'s Mail" on the front of the folder mailbox.

3. Repeat to make a mailbox for each family member, if desired. Use tape to hang each one in a different location in the house.

STEPS

1. Examine the postcards with your child. If you have some that have been previously mailed, point out the written messages, addresses, and stamps.

2. Invite her to fill out blank postcards using scribble-writing, drawing, and stickers as pretend postage stamps. Help her write the recipients' names for easier mail delivery.

3. Have her put the postcards in her mailbox to be mailed, then pretend to be a postal worker picking up the mail and delivering the postcards to the family members' mailboxes.

4. Take turns preparing postcards and playing the role of postal worker delivering them.

CAUTION! *Keep your toddler's fingers away from the scissors during mailbox making.*

SKILLS
LEARNED   colors   imagination   oral motor
development   sensory
development

Color Taste-Test Picnic

Indoor picnics were always a hit with my little ones, especially when we included a color taste test.

Messiness: 3
Prep Time: 10 minutes
Activity Time: 20 minutes

MATERIALS

Muffin pan

Fruits, vegetables, and finger foods, of the same color

Paring knife (optional)

Throw blanket

Plates and utensils (optional)

Napkins

TIP *Choose a color before your next grocery trip. Looking for foods of that color will keep your toddler entertained and even learning while shopping.*

PREP

1. Together with your toddler, choose a color for your taste test.

2. Fill each cup of the muffin pan with different finger foods of that color. Wash, peel, and cut foods into bite-size pieces, as needed.

3. Lay a blanket on the living room floor and place the muffin pan of finger foods, plates, utensils, and napkins in the center.

STEPS

1. Invite your toddler to join you for a taste-test picnic on the blanket on the floor.

2. Help him identify each food in the muffin pan and choose one to taste test.

3. Encourage mindful eating, asking your child to chew slowly and notice each food's taste and texture.

4. Repeat with each food in the muffin pan. Discuss which ones you each like or dislike.

CAUTION! *Keep sharp knives and utensils out of your toddler's reach. Choose foods that are appropriate for your child and always monitor for choking while he is eating.*

Eggs, Bacon & Pancakes Flip

Make some simple play food so your toddler can cook breakfast. She'll get valuable motor skill and counting practice while flipping and serving eggs, bacon, and pancakes.

Messiness: **2**
Prep Time: **5 minutes**
Activity Time: **10 minutes**

MATERIALS

Craft foam sheets, in white, yellow, red, brown, and tan

Scissors

Double-sided tape

Permanent markers, in red, brown, and/or black

Spatula

Frying pan, actual or toy

Plastic dishes and utensils, actual or toy

Small pom-poms, blue

TIP *Find an old frying pan, spatula, and plastic dishes at the thrift store or yard sales. Store them in a bin with your play food.*

PREP

Make pretend eggs, bacon, and pancakes. Here's how:

- **Fried eggs:** Cut fried egg–like oval shapes out of white foam and yolk-size circles out of yellow foam. Tape a yellow circle onto the center of each white shape.
- **Bacon:** Cut wavy strips, about two by six inches, out of brown and red foam. Draw irregular wavy lines on them with brown, red, and/or black permanent markers.
- **Pancakes:** Cut circles out of tan foam. Cut small butter-like squares out of yellow foam.

STEPS

1. Invite your toddler to make breakfast by using the spatula to cook and flip the eggs, bacon, and pancakes in the frying pan.

2. Add listening, memory, and counting practice by asking her to prepare you a specific number of each food. Have her use the spatula to transfer the food to a plate.

3. Add yellow squares of butter and blue pom-pom blueberries to the pancakes.

CAUTION! *Keep sharp scissors out of your toddler's reach. Skip the pom-poms and small foam pieces if your toddler is apt to put small objects in her mouth.*

Sprinkle Dough Celebration

Make this sweet-smelling, taste-safe playdough with your toddler for some celebration-themed sensory play.

Messiness: **4**
Prep Time: **None**
Activity Time: **20 minutes**

MATERIALS

1 (16-ounce) container white frosting

½ teaspoon vanilla extract (optional)

2¼ cups cornstarch

Mixing bowl

Wooden spoon

Vegetable oil (optional)

Sprinkles, colorful

Muffin pan (optional)

Cupcake liners, ideally silicone (optional)

Birthday cake candles (optional)

STEPS

1. Have your toddler help make playdough by first adding the frosting, vanilla (if using), and cornstarch to a mixing bowl, and then stirring the mixture with the wooden spoon until a dough starts to form and pulls away from the sides of the bowl.

2. Knead the dough until it reaches the desired playdough consistency, adding more cornstarch as needed. Knead in a tablespoon of vegetable oil at a time to soften it if it gets too dry.

3. Allow your child to knead some sprinkles into the dough. Then you can offer him a muffin pan, cupcake liners, and birthday candles for pretend play and cupcake making.

TIP *Make this activity a birthday tradition for your child. Or play pretend birthday just for fun!*

CAUTION! *While this homemade playdough is taste safe for curious toddlers, it is not intended for eating.*

fine motor skills	imagination	sensory development	visual spatial skills	SKILLS LEARNED

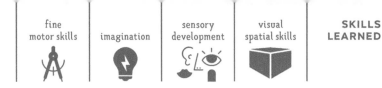

Winter Wonderland Play

Inspire some imaginative and sensory-rich winter wonderland play with just a few common household items.

Messiness: 2
Prep Time: **None**
Activity Time: **20 minutes**

MATERIALS

Large plastic tray

Aluminum foil

Cotton balls

Sequins or gems, silver and/or blue (optional)

Polyester pillow filling (optional)

Arctic animal toys or other toys

STEPS

1. Together with your toddler, cover the tray with aluminum foil to create a pretend ice-covered lake.

2. Provide her with some cotton balls, pieces of crinkled foil, sequins, gems, and polyester filling, if you have some, for arranging as snow and ice around the pretend lake.

3. Offer some plastic arctic animal toys, such as penguins, polar bears, and seals, for imaginative winter wonderland play.

TIP *Use any small toy figures you have if you don't have arctic animal toys.*

CAUTION! *Skip the small objects if your toddler still mouths objects during play.*

Indoor Penny Yard Sale

This is an activity my kids taught me. They gathered up a bunch of toys and set up a little pretend yard sale, all on their own!

Messiness: 2
Prep Time: **None**
Activity Time: 20 minutes

MATERIALS

Toys and stuffed animals

Small blank stickers

Marker

Pennies, real or toy

STEPS

1. Help your toddler gather various toys and stuffed animals for a pretend yard sale. Have him line them up along furniture and/or tables.

2. While he's gathering toys, use the marker to write a price (from 1¢ through 10¢) on each sticker.

3. Take turns shopping at the pretend yard sale, counting out pennies for payment.

TIP *Teach coins and their values to older toddlers or big kids by using various coins and making the price stickers 1¢, 5¢, 10¢, and 25¢.*

CAUTION! *Skip the coins if your toddler is apt to put small objects in his mouth. Try paper play money and dollar amounts on the price stickers instead.*

Make Your Own Movie Theater

Add some snacks and homemade tickets and you've got yourself an imaginative trip to the movie theater—right in your living room!

Messiness: 2
Prep Time: None
Activity Time: 30 minutes

MATERIALS

TV and movie

Construction paper

Scissors

Markers

Small star stickers

Small containers, for snacks

Drinks in sippy cups

Popcorn, candy, and snacks

Throw pillows

STEPS

1. Have your toddler choose a movie, and then help make a small rectangular movie ticket for each person, using construction paper, scissors, markers, and stickers. Encourage scribble-writing and the use of numbers for the movie time and cost.

2. Have her line up the drinks and various snacks (each in a different container) on a table near the entrance and place throw pillows on the floor for theater seats.

3. Invite her to the movies, taking her ticket and allowing her to choose snacks and a drink at the concession stand upon entering.

4. Turn the lights down, sit on the pillows, and enjoy your snacks while watching the movie together.

TIP *Add some early math learning by making simple sticker price tags (from 1¢ through 10¢) for the snacks at the concession stand and use pennies to pay for them.*

CAUTION! *Monitor your toddler closely for choking while eating snacks. Skip the popcorn if you suspect your toddler cannot chew it thoroughly.*

Under-the-Table Sea

This sea-themed activity takes a little setup, but your toddler can help and get some fine-motor-skill practice doing so. Having a magical sea to play in afterward makes it worth it!

Messiness: 3
Prep Time: None
Activity Time: 30 minutes

MATERIALS

Crepe paper streamers, in blue, green, and white

Tape

Dining table

String

Balloons, in blue and white, inflated

Ocean animal or ocean-themed toys

Snorkels and swimming goggles (optional)

STEPS

1. Have your toddler help rip crepe paper streamers into various lengths (one- to two-feet long). Tape them so they hang down from the underside of the dining table.

2. Use string and tape to hang some balloons from the underside of the table, making sure the string isn't more than a foot or so long. Place the remaining balloons on the floor under the table.

3. Together with your toddler, go on a hunt around the house for some ocean-themed toys, such as plastic ocean animal figures, bath toys, or stuffed animals, and place them under the table.

4. Grab snorkels and swimming goggles if you want and join your toddler under the table for some imaginative sea-themed play. Encourage lots of pretend swimming and sea animal toy identification.

CAUTION! *Never leave the play setup in place unsupervised, as the materials can pose strangulation and injury hazards.*

Robot-Activation Cuffs

The buttons on these crafted cuffs will help you and your little one sound and move like robots.

Messiness: 1
Prep Time: None
Activity Time: 20 minutes

MATERIALS

Scissors

Cardboard tube from a paper towel roll

Aluminum foil

Tape, ideally double-sided

Foam shape stickers

STEPS

1. Cut a three-inch ring off the cardboard tube, then cut across the ring to make a cuff. Repeat, for as many cuffs as you need.

2. Help your child wrap each cuff in aluminum foil. Use tape to secure the foil, as needed.

3. Have her add buttons to the cuffs by applying foam shape stickers.

4. Put the robot cuffs on and press the buttons to activate your robot voices and movements.

CAUTION! *Always keep your toddler away from sharp scissors and monitor closely with small foam stickers that she could choke on.*

SKILLS
LEARNED

fine
motor skills

imagination

language
development

social-emotional
development

Royal-Family Crowns

This fun crown craft puts an imaginative twist on learning about family relationships and vocabulary. And it's perfect to do with siblings!

Messiness: 2
Prep Time: 5 minutes
Activity Time: 30 minutes

MATERIALS

Scissors

1 or 2 cereal boxes

Aluminum foil

Tape, ideally
double-sided

Hole punch

Black permanent
marker

Self-adhesive
rhinestones

Stickers, ideally
sparkly or stars

Pipe cleaners

PREP

1. Cut the front and back off each cereal box, then cut each front/back piece in half lengthwise, making about equal-size strips.

2. Cut one long side of each strip into a scalloped, zigzag, or wavy edge.

STEPS

1. With your toddler, discuss the members of your family and their relationship titles (father, mother, sister, brother, grandma, grandpa, etc.). Decide who to make crowns for besides your toddler.

2. For each crown, help your child cover a cereal box strip entirely in aluminum foil. Use tape, as needed. Punch a hole in each end.

3. Use the permanent marker to write the family member's title on the front of each foil-covered crown strip. Say the letters and words aloud for your child while doing so.

4. Have your toddler decorate each crown strip with sparkly self-adhesive rhinestones and stickers.

5. Add a pipe cleaner to each punched hole. Then twist each crown's pipe cleaners together to make circular crowns appropriately sized for each wearer.

6. Wear the crowns while playing royal family or just for fun throughout the day. Address one another as "King Daddy," "Queen Mommy," "Prince Joey," and so on.

CAUTION! *Keep sharp scissors away from little toddler hands. And skip the small rhinestones altogether if your toddler is apt to put small objects in his mouth.*

Pet-Shelter Play

Gather up your child's stuffed animals for an imaginative play idea that also teaches about pet care, responsibility, and volunteering.

Messiness: 2
Prep Time: None
Activity Time: 30 minutes

MATERIALS

Various boxes, bins, and laundry baskets

Binder clips or utility clips (optional)

Throw pillows, blankets, or towels

Stuffed animals, such as dogs, cats, birds, fish, snakes, and lizards

Pet animal stickers (optional)

Washable markers (optional)

Index cards (optional)

Tape

Pipe cleaners, or ribbons

Blank hang tags

Pom-poms

Small plastic containers and scoops

STEPS

1. Discuss with your child some different types of pets and what they need, such as food, water, vet care, exercise, comfort, and love. Explain what shelters are by saying something like, "Shelters provide those things for pets who don't have a place to live, until they can find them loving homes."

2. Help her gather boxes, bins, and laundry baskets, and line them up on their sides to make pretend animal crates. You can also make stacked crates by clipping box sides together. Add throw pillows, blankets, or towels to the crates.

3. Invite your toddler to gather a variety of stuffed animals, ideally typical pet animals, and place each one in a crate.

4. You can help her identify the animals and make labels for each using animal stickers, washable markers, and index cards. Allow your toddler to match each label with its matching pet crate and tape it on.

5. Help her make collars for appropriate animals (such as dogs, cats, and bunnies) using pipe cleaners or ribbons. Have her name them and help her make name tags for their collars using hang tags.

6. Together, play pretend animal shelter, caring for and adopting pets. Use pom-poms and small plastic containers and scoops for pretend food and water. Take turns interviewing one another for adoptions, emphasizing caring, responsibility, and each pet's specific needs.

CAUTION! *If you stack boxes or bins, make sure they are safely secured so they do not fall, and take them down after play is finished.*

Mini Home Office

It's becoming more and more common for today's toddlers to have adults in their lives who work from home. Set up this pretend home office to inspire some imaginative work-at-home play and letter learning, too.

Messiness: 1
Prep Time: **None**
Activity Time: 20 minutes

MATERIALS

Cardboard box, medium-size

Glue stick, or tape

Construction paper, white

Stickers

Washable markers

Old computer keyboard and mouse (optional)

Alphabet and number stickers (optional)

Aluminum foil (optional)

Various office supplies, such as pencils, notepads, sticky notes, a clipboard, envelopes, and a calculator

STEPS

1. Help your toddler make a computer screen on the cardboard box by gluing a slightly smaller rectangle of white construction paper onto one side. Have him decorate the paper screen with stickers and washable markers.

2. Position the box computer on a table with the keyboard and mouse, if you have them. If not, make a pretend keyboard by drawing small squares on a rectangle of cardboard, then have your toddler stick the sticker letters and numbers inside the squares. You can wrap an empty juice box in aluminum foil to make a pretend mouse.

3. Place various office supplies around the computer and allow your toddler free time to play and explore his new mini home office.

4. Add learning by having your toddler press letter keys on the keyboard to spell his name or a word you've written on paper. Or, if you have a calculator, call out numbers for him to find and press.

CAUTION! *Always keep your toddler away from sharp scissors. Make sure to skip small office supplies if your toddler is apt to put objects in his mouth.*

Dress Up Dice

Invite your little one to play the classic play favorite, dress up, in a fun new way—with dice!

Messiness: 2
Prep Time: 10 minutes
Activity Time: 20 minutes

MATERIALS

Various dress up items, such as clothes, hats, scarves, sunglasses, and jewelry

Large plastic bin

Cardboard box, square, small- to medium-size

White paper

Scissors (optional)

Tape

Black permanent marker

CAUTION! *Choose dress up items appropriate for your child, limiting small items if he is apt to put them in his mouth. Never allow unsupervised play with dress up items, as some can be strangulation and injury hazards.*

PREP

1. If you don't have one already, collect various dress up items in a large bin. Check thrift stores and yard sales for inexpensive options.

2. Wrap a square cardboard box with white paper, using scissors and tape, as needed.

3. With the permanent marker, draw (or write) a different dress up item, corresponding with the ones in your bin, on each side of the dice, such as a baseball cap, a dress, a scarf, sunglasses, and a necklace.

STEPS

1. Have your toddler roll the dice and put on the dress up item showing on the dice. For example, if it shows a scarf, he must choose a scarf from the bin and put it on.

2. Have him repeat, rolling the dice and putting on multiple dress up items. Allow him to try putting on and removing items on his own before stepping in to help. Expect giggles when multiple items get layered!

3. To take the items off, have him roll the dice again. This might add some challenge and silliness if it is in a different order than how the item was put on.

4. Add more fun and connection by taking turns rolling and putting on items, and then play pretend characters, with silly voices, after you're all dressed up.

Salad Bar Memory Game

Set up a simple pretend salad bar for your toddler to play this unique salad-making memory game. She'll get lots of fine-motor-skill practice playing this game, too.

Messiness: 4
Prep Time: None
Activity Time: 30 minutes

MATERIALS

Tissue paper, in shades of green

Construction paper, orange

Craft foam sheets, green

Pipe cleaners, red

Pom-poms, black

Safety scissors

Multiple plastic containers or bins

Various tongs, or serving spoons

Plastic dishes and utensils, real or toy

CAUTION! *Skip small supplies if your toddler mouths objects during play. Always monitor closely when she practices with scissors.*

STEPS

1. Have your toddler help name and describe typical salad ingredients, such as green lettuce, shredded carrots, round sliced cucumbers, red bell peppers, and round black olives.

2. Have her help make various pretend salad ingredients. Try these easy, toddler-friendly ideas:

   - **Lettuce:** Rip green tissue paper into lettuce-size pieces.
   - **Shredded carrots:** Use safety scissors to snip strips of orange construction paper.
   - **Sliced cucumbers:** Sort green circles out of various foam shapes or cut some out of green foam sheets.
   - **Bell pepper rings:** Bend and twist red pipe cleaners into rings.
   - **Black olives:** Sort out black pom-poms from other colors.

3. Place each ingredient in a container and line them up, along with tongs and/or serving spoons.

4. Order a salad with certain ingredients for your toddler to make for you. Have her use tongs and/or spoons to place each ingredient in order on a plate.

5. Pretend to eat, practice manners, and then sort the ingredients back into their containers before playing again.

| early literacy | fine motor skills | imagination | sensory development | shapes and letters | social-emotional development | **SKILLS LEARNED** |

ABC Baby Doll Bath

Little girls *and* boys benefit immensely from playing with dolls. Caring for a baby doll helps them practice social skills and develop empathy. This baby doll activity gets your toddler in the bathtub for some alphabet fun!

Messiness: 2
Prep Time: 5 minutes
Activity Time: 30 minutes

MATERIALS

Bath crayon, or washable crayons

Water-friendly baby doll

Bathtub, water, and soap

Small sponge, or washcloth

Towels

TIP *You can also do this activity using a sink or large bin of soapy water instead of the bathtub, if desired.*

PREP

Without your toddler seeing, use bath crayons to write the letters of the alphabet randomly on the doll's body. Test the crayons on a small spot first, to make sure the mark cleans off entirely. And test each type of crayon to see which works best on your doll.

STEPS

1. Add some water and soap for bubbles to the bathtub and help your toddler get in.

2. Give him the doll to join him in the bath. Act surprised by the letters the doll must have written on herself.

3. Have him use a small sponge to scrub the letters off the doll, identifying each letter while doing so. If he can already identify letters, call them out one at a time for him to find and clean off.

4. Encourage him to be gentle, saying "Be gentle. Remember, it's a baby."

5. Have towels ready to wrap the baby and your toddler in when they're done with their ABC bath.

CAUTION! *Always supervise your child when he is in the bathtub or playing with water.*

Florist Fun

Grab some artificial flowers from the dollar store to inspire pretend flower arranging, social skills practice, and some number and color learning, too.

Messiness: 1
Prep Time: 10 minutes
Activity Time: 15 minutes

MATERIALS

5 different recyclable containers, such as oatmeal canisters, formula cans, and cut-off milk cartons

Scissors

Tape

Construction paper, in various colors

Washable markers

Artificial flowers, in various colors

Large basket

CAUTION! *Keep your toddler away from the sharp scissors during prep.*

PREP

1. Gather and prepare the containers, cleaning and cutting off the tops, as needed. Use tape to cover each container in a different color of construction paper.

2. Use a washable marker to write a different number, 1 through 5, on each container and line them up on the table.

3. Use scissors to separate any flowers in bunches and trim their stems to be proportionate to the containers. Place them in a large basket on the table next to the container vases.

STEPS

1. Discuss how florists arrange (or place) flowers in vases for people to buy for their home or to give as a gift.

2. Help your toddler identify the color and number on each vase and the colors of the flowers.

3. Order flowers of a certain color or in a certain-color container for her to arrange for you. Practice manners and polite conversation.

4. Add some learning by challenging her to use the numbers on the sides of the vases as a guide to put the correct number of flowers in each. Or have her sort the flowers into their matching-color vases.

Weather Station Play

What better profession for pretend play on a rainy day than meteorologist? Your toddler will observe the weather outside, and then pretend to report the weather using a real map!

Messiness: 2
Prep Time: **None**
Activity Time: 20 minutes

MATERIALS

Tape

Paper map

TV or computer (optional)

Crayons

Blank labels, or sticky notes

TIP *Add to the fun by recording your toddler's weather report with your smartphone and letting him watch himself afterward.*

STEPS

1. Have your child join you on the porch or at a window to observe and discuss the weather outside. Use weather words, such as *rainy, windy, snowy, cloudy, warm,* and *cold.*

2. Tape a map onto the wall, then examine and discuss it together. Point out your location, if possible. Explain that meteorologists use maps to show the weather in different areas. Watch a short weather report together on TV or online, if possible.

3. Help your child make weather stickers using crayons to draw weather symbols, such as the sun, snowflakes, lightning bolts, clouds, and raindrops, on the labels or sticky notes. It's okay if he simply scribble-draws on some while you draw symbols on others.

4. Have your toddler add the weather stickers on the map any way he wants to make it look like a meteorologist's weather map.

5. Demonstrate how to play meteorologist, pointing at the map and talking about the weather each sticker shows. Let him try playing pretend meteorologist, helping him as needed.

- 4 -
GET YOUR WIGGLES OUT

Toddlers move constantly. Who can blame them? They have a whole lot of motor skills to learn in a short amount of time! But that seemingly constant motion can be quite the challenge when you're in a small house or apartment or are inside the entire day.

The activities in this chapter not only allow your toddler to move, but also encourage new and beneficial movements. Toddlers need a variety of movements for proper sensory regulation and motor skill development. And you need to help them expel some of that energy so you can get through your day and have some fun with your toddler, too.

Pizza Delivery

Get your toddler making and delivering pretend pizzas for a fun carrying and balancing challenge.

Messiness: 2
Prep Time: None
Activity Time: 20 minutes

MATERIALS

Pom-poms, in red, green, yellow, and brown

4 small plastic containers

Paper plate

Cardboard pizza box, or other cardboard box

STEPS

1. Have your toddler sort the pom-poms by color into separate containers. Explain how they will be the pizza ingredients: red are pepperoni, green are green peppers, yellow are cheese, and brown are sausage.

2. Have him make a pizza by placing pom-pom ingredients on a paper plate crust and carefully transfer it into the pizza box without letting the ingredients fall off.

3. Then challenge him to deliver the pizza to another location in the house, also without any ingredients falling off the pizza inside.

4. Repeat, for more pizza making, carrying, balancing, and pizza delivery fun.

5. Add to the challenge by ordering specific ingredients on a pizza you would like delivered to you across the room.

TIP *Save the box after an actual pizza delivery, if possible. Or see if you can get a new, clean one from your favorite pizza place. If an actual pizza box isn't possible, improvise with any cardboard box that can hold a paper plate pizza.*

CAUTION! *Any activity with small pom-poms may not be appropriate for your toddler if he mouths objects during play.*

Farm Animal Roundup

Get ready for fun farm animal sounds! Your little one will love pretending to be each animal while she rounds them up into the laundry basket corral.

Messiness: 1
Prep Time: None
Activity Time: 20 minutes

MATERIALS

Farm animal toys or stuffed animals

Laundry basket

STEPS

1. Invite your toddler to help you gather up a bunch of farm animal toys. Collect them in a laundry basket as you go.

2. Identify each animal and discuss and practice its sounds and movements. Try these animal ideas:

   - **Cow:** moo while pretending to chew cud and sway while walking lazily.
   - **Pig:** grunt and oink while rolling across the "mud" floor.
   - **Chicken:** cluck and jut your chin in and out while walking with high knees.
   - **Horse:** neigh while galloping and running.
   - **Cat:** meow and purr while walking on hands and knees or pouncing.
   - **Dog:** bark and yip while walking excitedly on hands and knees.

3. Have your toddler cover her eyes while you hide the animals around the room or house. Then place the empty laundry basket on the floor as the pretend farm animal corral.

4. Have your child round up the farm animals, making each animal's sounds and movements while bringing them back to the corral.

TIP *If you don't have farm animals, any animal toys could work. Simply call the basket a zoo enclosure instead.*

Recycling Collector

Set up a simple pretend recycling center for some beneficial motor skill work and even some sorting practice, too.

Messiness: 2
Prep Time: 5 minutes
Activity Time: 15 minutes

MATERIALS

Recycling bin, or large plastic bin

Cardboard, paper, and plastic recycled materials, such as boxes, paper scraps, and plastic water bottles

3 medium plastic bins

Toy wagon, or laundry basket and belt

PREP

1. Place a recycling bin on the floor and add half of the recyclables.

2. Line the three medium bins up in a faraway location in the house. Place a cardboard recyclable in one, a paper recyclable in another, and a plastic recyclable in the last one.

STEPS

1. Have your toddler pretend to be a recycling collector by pulling her wagon over to the recycling bin and transferring the recyclables into it. Discuss each recyclable material (cardboard, paper, and plastic).

2. Have her pull the wagon to the recycling center where you've placed the bins, and sort them based on the materials already in each bin.

3. Repeat with the other recyclables for more imaginative pulling and sorting play.

TIP *No toy wagon? Hook a belt through a handle on a laundry basket for your toddler to pull like a wagon instead.*

CAUTION! *Only use clean, kid-friendly recyclables; no glass or sharp cans.*

A Movement-Filled Metamorphosis

Help your toddler experience a metamorphosis—from a crawling caterpillar, to a calming chrysalis, and, finally, to a flying butterfly.

Messiness: 1
Prep Time: **None**
Activity Time: 10 minutes

MATERIALS

Long-sleeve shirt, for your toddler

5 sheets construction paper, green

Throw blanket

2 lightweight square scarves

Safety pins, or clips

CAUTION! *Make sure your toddler's head is out of the blanket at all times, and don't wrap the blanket too tight. Also, keep your toddler away from loose pins and small clips since they can be injury or choking hazards.*

STEPS

1. Have your toddler wear a long-sleeve shirt. Then, together with your child, loosely crumple each sheet of construction paper and place these "leaves" on the floor around the room. While doing so, discuss caterpillars and their metamorphosis (or process of changing) into butterflies.

2. Have him pretend to be a caterpillar, keeping his arms and legs together and crawling on elbows and knees around the room to munch the leaves.

3. Explain how eating them made him grow and now it's time to form a chrysalis. Help him wrap the blanket snugly around his body, keeping his head out.

4. Have him close his eyes and take some calming deep breaths for a moment of mindfulness in the chrysalis.

5. Have him wiggle one arm out and attach a scarf butterfly wing to his shirt, pinning one corner at the shoulder and another corner at the end of the sleeve. Repeat, pinning the other scarf wing onto the other shoulder and sleeve.

6. Help him wiggle and stretch to completely free himself from the chrysalis. Encourage him to test his wings by flying around the house.

gross
motor skills

imagination

sensory
development

visual
spatial skills

Stormy Seas

Sensory development isn't just about touching textures with your hands. It's about movement, too! Give your child's vestibular sensory system (which controls her sense of movement and balance) some beneficial input with this rocky boat ride.

Messiness: 1
Prep Time: None
Activity Time: 15 minutes

MATERIALS

Couch cushions and/or pillows

Laundry basket

Heavyweight cardboard tube, or broom handle

STEPS

1. Together with your child, place a large sea of couch cushions and/or pillows on the floor.

2. Place the laundry basket on top and in the center of the sea. Help your toddler get inside the boat.

3. Give her the cardboard tube to use as an oar and sing "Row, Row, Row Your Boat" together while you rock the boat gently from behind.

4. Pretend there is a stormy sea and shake and tilt the boat from side to side. Make sure the cushions and/or pillows remain on each side to cushion potential falls.

5. Have her use the oar, pushing one end down into the sea to try to steady the boat.

6. Go back and forth between calm and stormy seas and their movements.

CAUTION! *Make sure the floor is adequately covered with cushions and/or pillows to prevent injury if your toddler tips out.*

Kid-Size Connect the Dots

Get your little one expelling some energy and counting, too, with this giant connect the dots indoor-play idea.

Messiness: 2
Prep Time: 5 minutes
Activity Time: 10 minutes

MATERIALS

Painter's tape

Paper plates

Washable marker

Stopwatch (optional)

PREP

1. Tape paper plates onto the floor to create a dot-to-dot path throughout the house. Leave greater distance between plates if you want to make the activity more challenging.

2. Use the washable marker to write a number on each plate, starting with 1 at the beginning of the path and continuing in sequential order.

STEPS

1. Practice with your toddler first, walking the connect the dots path, identifying the numbers and counting as you go.

2. Return to the beginning and challenge him to connect the dots on his own.

3. You can add to the fun and learning by having him repeat the challenge multiple times as quickly as he can, timing him each time.

CAUTION! *Make sure to secure the paper plates down to the floor with tape as they could be slippery and cause a fall. Painter's tape shouldn't leave any residue on the floor, but test it if you haven't tried it before.*

SKILLS
LEARNED | gross
motor skills | numbers and
counting | visual
spatial skills

123

Beach Ball Bowling

Can't get to the beach? Get your beachwear on anyway for an active beach-themed bowling game!

Messiness: 2
Prep Time: 5 minutes
Activity Time: 10 minutes

MATERIALS

Painter's tape

1 or 2 beach towels

10 plastic cups, ideally colorful

Black permanent marker

Beachwear and accessories, such as swimsuit, flip-flops, sunglasses, and beach hat

Beach ball, inflated

PREP

1. Tape a beach towel onto the floor (or two towels in a row) for the bowling lane.

2. Use the permanent marker to write a number from 1 to 10 on each cup.

3. At one end of the beach towel, place 10 small pieces of tape on the floor in a triangular bowling-pin pattern to indicate where each pin should be placed.

STEPS

1. Dress your toddler in her beachwear and invite her to the beach bowling alley.

2. Help her identify and count the numbers on the cup pins as you set them up on the tape marks on the floor.

3. Have her stand at the other end of the towel and roll the beach ball down the towel alley to bowl down the pins. Help her identify the numbers on the pins she knocks down and count them as she puts them back in place. Repeat, taking turns, if desired.

CAUTION! *Make sure to secure the towels to the floor with tape as they could be slippery and cause a fall. Painter's tape shouldn't leave any residue on the floor, but test it if you haven't tried it before.*

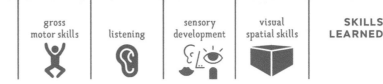

Twist & Turn Track

Crawling on the floor pushing a toy vehicle is incredibly beneficial for your toddler's motor skills and sensory development. Here's a fun way to get him racing around the floor and practicing listening, too.

Messiness: 2
Prep Time: 5 minutes
Activity Time: 10 minutes

MATERIALS

Painter's tape

Toy car

PREP

Apply a long painter's tape line on the floor that twists and turns in different directions and goes from room to room, if possible.

STEPS

1. Have your toddler start at one end and drive his toy car along the track.

2. Help him identify left and right turns as he goes along the track.

3. Make it a silly game by calling out "Turn!" at random for him to turn the car around and start going back in the other direction.

4. Include learning about fast and slow by calling each out at random for him to adjust his car's speed.

CAUTION! *Painter's tape shouldn't leave any residue on the floor, but test it if you haven't tried it before.*

Bubble-Hop Dance Party

Inspire creative dancing and practice listening skills with this twist on a freeze dance party.

Messiness: 1
Prep Time: **None**
Activity Time: 10 minutes

MATERIALS

Painter's tape

Bubble Wrap

Music

STEPS

1. Tape a square of Bubble Wrap onto the floor with painter's tape. Invite your toddler to stand on it.

2. Explain the bubble-hop dance party rules: Dance to the music while standing on the Bubble Wrap. When the music stops, switch to hopping. When it starts again, start dancing again. And so on, for the entire song, without stepping off the Bubble Wrap!

3. Play upbeat music and randomly stop and restart it while your toddler dances and hops.

CAUTION! *Make sure to secure the Bubble Wrap down to the floor with tape as it could be slippery and cause a fall. Painter's tape shouldn't leave any residue on the floor, but test it if you haven't tried it before.*

Snow-Machine Science

Can't go outside to play in the snow? Make it snow inside using simple physics to make a super-fun snow machine. Your toddler will love seeing it snow and running around to shovel it, too.

Messiness: 3
Prep Time: None
Activity Time: 20 minutes

MATERIALS

Small plastic food-storage container, or plastic cup

Duct tape

Yardstick

Pom-poms, in white, silver, and/or light blue

Canned food item

Kid's snow shovel, or broom

STEPS

1. Position the plastic container upside down and tape the yardstick across the bottom of it with one end even with the edge of the container and the other end extending off the other side of the container.

2. Flip it over and have your child fill the container with pom-pom snow.

3. Help him position the canned food item on its side, underneath, and about six inches in from the container-free end of the yardstick.

4. Test it yourself first by standing alongside the yardstick (not at either end where you could get hit) and stomping on the container-free end to make the container end rise up. Share in your child's excitement when the snow launches into the air!

5. Have him use a toy shovel to gather the snow and refill the container. Then help him set the lever snow machine up again and try stomping this time.

6. Have him shovel the snow and repeat making snow fly indoors.

CAUTION! *Make sure your child is away from the rising end of the yardstick when you stomp.*

SKILLS
LEARNED

gross
motor skills

visual
spatial skills

Soccer Sweep

No worries over kicked balls breaking things with this calmer version of soccer! But it will still have your toddler moving throughout the house, strengthening motor skills and practicing hand-eye coordination.

Messiness: 1
Prep Time: None
Activity Time: 10 minutes

MATERIALS

Laundry basket

Kid's broom, or full-size broom

Soccer ball, or other large ball

STEPS

1. Together with your child, position the laundry basket on its side on the floor to serve as a soccer goal.

2. Move to a different location in the house; the farther away, the more challenging the activity.

3. Have her use a broom to sweep and roll the soccer ball through the house and into the laundry-basket goal.

4. Repeat, from different locations in the house. Do a silly celebration dance whenever she makes a soccer sweep goal.

TIP *You can set up another laundry basket and play as teams, trying to get the soccer ball in the other team's goal.*

Puzzle Hide-and-Seek

Transform a typical toddler puzzle into an active indoor game with this simple hide-and-seek trick.

Messiness: 2
Prep Time: None
Activity Time: 10 minutes

MATERIALS

Toddler puzzle

STEPS

1. Look at the puzzle together and discuss what you see.

2. Have your toddler cover her eyes while you hide the puzzle pieces around the room.

3. Have her run to find a puzzle piece, bring it to the puzzle, and place it in its spot.

4. Have her repeat this until all pieces have been found and the puzzle is complete.

CAUTION! *Make sure your puzzle has toddler-friendly pieces that aren't too small.*

SKILLS
LEARNED

gross
motor skills

social–emotional
development

visual
spatial skills

Egg-Gather Relay

Get a group of kids moving and working together with a fun indoor relay race.

Messiness: 2
Prep Time: 5 minutes
Activity Time: 20 minutes

MATERIALS

8 brown paper
lunch bags

24 plastic Easter eggs

2 egg cartons

Stopwatch (optional)

TIP *Not enough kids for two teams? Set up the relay with just one row of four nests. Time them as they do it together multiple times or as each child does it to see who's fastest.*

PREP

1. Fold and crumple the edges of each lunch bag down to make nests. Place three plastic eggs in each one.

2. Set up two rows of four nests on the floor with a good amount of space between the rows and about six feet between the nests within each row.

STEPS

1. Divide the kids into two teams and give each team an egg carton.

2. Explain the rules of the egg-gather relay: When you hear "GO!" run to the first nest, gather the eggs out of it, carry them back as quickly as possible without dropping any, and place each one in your team's carton. Then another team member runs to the next nest, gathers the eggs, carries them back, and places them in the carton. And so on, until all eggs have been gathered. The first team to fill their carton wins.

3. Count down from three and say "GO!" to start the relay race.

4. Cheer both teams on as they run and gather eggs and giggle along when they struggle carrying three eggs at once.

RAINY DAY
FUN TOGETHER

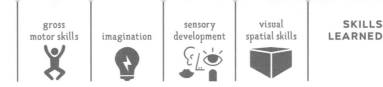
Snowplow Rider

Even when living in a little apartment, my toddlers had at least one indoor ride-on toy. They are great for getting toddler muscles moving, practicing motor skills, and providing unique movements beneficial to the sensory system. Here's a snowy way to get your little one riding indoors.

Messiness: 2
Prep Time: 5 minutes
Activity Time: 20 minutes

MATERIALS

Cardboard, a large rectangle

Utility knife, or scissors

Indoor ride-on toy, or kid's snow shovel or broom

Cable ties and/or duct tape

Paper, white, printer or lined

Painter's tape (optional)

PREP

1. Cut a cardboard rectangle a few inches larger than the front of your child's ride-on toy.

2. Use cable ties and/or duct tape to attach the horizontal cardboard rectangle onto the front of the ride-on toy, with the bottom near the floor like a snowplow. Use the utility knife or scissors to add holes for the cable ties, as needed.

STEPS

1. Have your toddler help make snowballs by crumpling up sheets of white paper. Have him strew them on the floor throughout house.

2. Invite him to drive his snowplow ride-on toy and plow the snow to a specific spot in the house. Use painter's tape to mark the spot on the floor, if desired.

TIP *No indoor ride-on toy? Be adventurous and bring in a small outdoor one. Just use a damp cloth to clean it up, if needed. Or use a toy snow shovel or broom for your child to pretend to shovel the snow instead.*

CAUTION! *Keep the sharp utility knife and scissors out of your toddler's reach during prep. Stay near your toddler and assist, as needed, while he rides on the ride-on toy.*

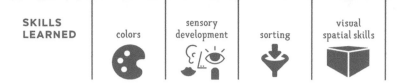
Sticky-Finish Color Sort

When my youngest had occupational therapy as a toddler, his therapist would teach us fun activities to help regulate his sensory system. This often included having him climb on and off the couch, over and over. Here's a fun way to get your toddler climbing and work on some color recognition too.

Messiness: 2
Prep Time: 10 minutes
Activity Time: 15 minutes

MATERIALS

2 long cardboard tubes from wrapping paper rolls, of equal length, with grooves on each end

Stapler and staples

Masking tape, wide

Construction paper, 1 sheet to match each ball color

2 canned food items

Ball-pit balls, in a bin

PREP

1. With the tubes side by side and the groove aligned where they touch, staple them together at each end. Reinforce one grooved side with tape, as needed, but leave the other grooved side tape-free for the ramp.

2. Make a finish line across the room from the couch, parallel to the couch, by taping the differently colored sheets of construction paper down, end to end, on the floor.

3. Place a canned food item on each end of the finish line. Run a long length of tape, sticky side facing the couch, from one can to the other.

4. Place the bin of balls on the couch.

STEPS

1. Have your toddler climb onto the couch, choose a ball, and then find its matching color along the sticky finish line.

2. Demonstrate how to prop one end of the ramp up on the couch and adjust the other end on the floor toward the matching color.

3. Have her place the ball in the groove at the top of the ramp and let it go to roll down the ramp, across the floor, and stick to the sticky finish line. Celebrate if it hits its matching color.

4. Have your toddler repeat it on her own, adjusting the ramp as needed to direct each ball toward its matching color at the sticky finish line.

CAUTION! *Stay nearby and assist your toddler, as needed, while she is climbing to prevent falls. This activity may not be suitable for your toddler if she isn't a confident climber.*

SKILLS
LEARNED

language
development

sensory
development

visual
spatial skills

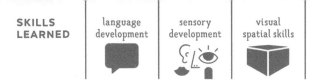

Sticky Sensory Path

Create an indoor sensory walk with your toddler. He'll love exploring the textures and materials while making it, and will enjoy walking along the finished path, too.

Messiness: 4
Prep Time: 5 minutes
Activity Time: 20 minutes

MATERIALS

Painter's tape

Contact paper

Materials of various textures, such as cotton balls, Bubble Wrap, crinkled aluminum foil, pom-poms, drinking straws, and thin sponges

PREP

Tape a long length of contact paper, sticky-side up, onto the floor.

STEPS

1. Invite your toddler to help press textured materials, one at a time, onto the sticky contact paper path.

2. Have him walk along the sensory path to feel each texture under his feet.

3. Ask him to describe what his feet feel as he walks the path. Encourage descriptive words like *soft, bumpy, hard, scratchy,* and *sticky.*

TIP *Want a path you can keep and reuse? Glue materials onto heavyweight paper plates you can tape to the floor instead.*

CAUTION! *Skip any small materials if your toddler is apt to put them in her mouth. And stay nearby to assist your toddler, if needed, as she walks along the path.*

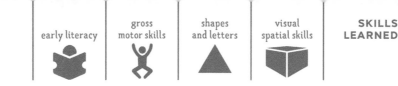

Alphabet Balloon Ball

Every kid loves the simple game of keeping a balloon in the air. Introduce this fun game to your toddler, but with some alphabet practice woven in.

Messiness: 0
Prep Time: **None**
Activity Time: 10 minutes

MATERIALS

Balloon, inflated

STEPS

1. Explain the rules of alphabet balloon ball to your child: Tap the balloon back and forth with your hands. Say the next letter in the alphabet each time you tap it. Don't let it touch the floor!

2. Toss the balloon up into the air and call out "A!" as you tap it upward with your hand.

3. Encourage your toddler to then tap the balloon upward and call out "B!"

4. Again, tap the balloon upward and call out "C!" Continue, taking turns tapping and calling out letters.

5. When the balloon hits the floor, start back at "A" and see if you can get through more letters.

TIP *If your toddler doesn't know the alphabet yet, play this game using counting instead. Or just play the old-fashioned way by trying to keep it in the air.*

CAUTION! *Never allow unsupervised play with balloons or leave uninflated balloons within your toddler's reach, as they can be a choking hazard.*

SKILLS
LEARNED

gross
motor skills

language
development

problem-
solving

visual
spatial skills

Over, Under & Through

Help your child better understand the concepts of over, under, and through with an action-packed obstacle course.

Messiness: 3
Prep Time: 10 minutes
Activity Time: 20 minutes

MATERIALS

String or yarn

Dining table

Painter's tape

Coffee table

2 couch cushions

2 dining chairs

Hula-Hoop

Stopwatch (optional)

PREP

Set up an obstacle course using materials from around your house. Alternate between obstacles requiring your toddler to go over, under, and through. Try one of these easy ideas:

- **Through the Table Spiderweb:** Wind and tie string around the legs of a dining table to make a spiderweb for crawling through.
- **Over the Tape Lines:** Make a series of painter's tape lines on the floor for jumping over.
- **Under the Coffee Table Crawl:** Set up a coffee table for crawling under.
- **Over the Cushion Crawl:** Stack a couple couch cushions on the floor for climbing over.
- **Through the Hula-Hoop:** Tie an upright Hula-Hoop between two dining chairs for crawling through.
- **Under the Tape Lines:** Apply painter's tape from one wall to the other across a hallway for ducking or crawling under.

STEPS

1. Have your toddler follow your lead and practice each obstacle, emphasizing the concepts of over, under, and through as you go.

2. Let her try the obstacle course on her own. Prompt her with "over," "under," and "through" as she goes. Stay close by to offer a hand for assistance and safety.

3. Add to the fun by timing your toddler with a stopwatch, if desired.

TIP *Adjust the number of obstacles for the age and ability of your toddler. Keep it to three or so obstacles for younger toddlers, and add more for older children.*

CAUTION! *Check all obstacles carefully prior to play, ensuring they are stable and free of hazards. Stay near your toddler during the activity, and never leave the obstacles in place when not supervising play, as the materials can be strangulation, tripping, and falling hazards.*

SKILLS
LEARNED

gross
motor skills

imagination

language
development

visual
spatial skills

Indoor Rainstorm

Use a toddler bedsheet for some rainstorm-themed parachute play on a day that's too rainy to go outside. Plus, those little arms will get a workout!

Messiness: 3
Prep Time: None
Activity Time: 10 minutes

MATERIALS

Toddler bedsheet, or small blanket

Pom-poms, in blue and silver

STEPS

1. Together with your toddler, spread the sheet out on the floor and place a bunch of pom-poms in the center.

2. Standing at each end of the sheet, grab the corners and lift at the same time.

3. Say, "It's starting to sprinkle," and encourage him to join you in gently shaking the sheet to make the raindrops start to move and bounce.

4. Tell him, "It's starting to rain harder now!" as you shake the sheet more vigorously and watch the raindrops bounce and fly into the air.

5. Continue, randomly making the rain lighter and stronger. Use lots of rainy-weather words, such as *drizzle, sprinkle, pour,* and *storm.*

TIP *No pom-poms? Crumple pieces of blue paper up to use instead.*

CAUTION! *Skip the pom-poms if your little one is likely to put them in his mouth.*

Stairstep Sock Ball

Make laundry duty more fun (and get your toddler helping match socks) with a simple and safe sock ball game!

Messiness: 2
Prep Time: **None**
Activity Time: 20 minutes

MATERIALS

Washable marker

5 sticky notes

5 plastic bins, medium-size

Socks, in a laundry basket

TIP *No stairs? Or worried about stair safety? Line the bins up on the floor, progressively farther away. Or line them up along the couch instead.*

STEPS

1. Together with your toddler, use the washable marker and sticky notes to label each plastic bin with a different number (1 through 5). Have him help place the bins on the first five steps of stairs, with bin number 1 on the bottom step and bin number 5 on the fifth step.

2. Challenge your toddler to find a matching pair of socks in the laundry basket. Help him ball them up together by placing them on top of each other, rolling them together from the toes up, then folding the opening of the outside sock back over them.

3. Have him stand at the bottom of the stairs and toss the sock ball into the bins and call out the number on the bin it lands in.

4. Repeat, matching socks, balling them up, playing sock ball, and calling out numbers until all of the socks are matched.

5. Try making it more challenging by calling out numbers for him to aim for.

6. After play, help him climb up and down the stairs to retrieve the sock balls, one at a time.

CAUTION! *Stay close by and assist your toddler, as needed, while climbing up and down stairs.*

Gone Fishing—for Shapes!

Get your wiggly toddler working those arms and practicing hand-eye coordination by fishing for shapes.

Messiness: 2
Prep Time: 10 minutes
Activity Time: 15 minutes

MATERIALS

String, about 2 feet long

Duct tape, or craft adhesive (optional)

Ruler

Magnet

Paper clips

Craft foam shapes

Small plastic containers, one for each shape

Shallow bin

PREP

1. Tie or tape the string to the end of the ruler. Tie or tape a magnet onto the other end of the string.

2. Put a paper clip on each foam shape.

3. Place a different shape in each plastic container and set the containers on the opposite side of the room.

STEPS

1. Have your toddler dump the foam shapes into the shallow bin.

2. Give her the fishing pole to fish for a shape, allowing the magnet to catch it by its metal paper clip.

3. Help her identify and sort the shape into the container across the room with the matching shape.

4. Allow her to continue fishing for shapes and sorting the ones she catches into the containers.

TIP *Craft foam shapes come in many themes, such as letters, numbers, farm animals, and sea life. Try fishing and sorting foam shapes you have on hand or buy some specific to your child's interests or learning.*

CAUTION! *Skip this activity if your toddler is apt to put the small shapes in her mouth as they can be a choking hazard.*

- 5 -
QUIET TIME

Every mama needs a break once in a while. But when you're a mom to an active toddler, you have to be on *all the time* just to ensure your little one's safety. It can be exhausting!

While the activities in this chapter still require your supervision, they were designed to capture your toddler's attention, encourage focused learning, and, for the most part, require simple or even no interaction from you—which gives you some time to observe your toddler at work and pat yourself on the back for adding some fun learning to the day.

SKILLS
LEARNED

colors

science

sensory
development

shapes
and letters

Circles of Light & Color

Make a simple light box for your toddler to explore circles, primary colors, and even the basic science of light and color.

Messiness: 2
Prep Time: 10 minutes
Activity Time: 10 minutes

MATERIALS

Tape

Large, clear shallow plastic bin, with lid

Wax paper

100-count clear mini string light set

Utility knife (optional)

Circular objects, various sizes, such as painter's tape, jar lids, and bowls

Black permanent marker

Translucent plastic file folders, in primary colors of red, yellow, and blue

Scissors

PREP

1. Use tape to line the underside of the bin's lid with wax paper.

2. Place the string of lights inside the bin, allowing the plug end of the cord to remain out over the side. Secure the lid on the bin. (If the lid doesn't work well due to the cord, you can use a utility knife to cut a small notch out of the edge of the bin to accommodate the cord.) Plug the cord in.

3. Use the circular objects and the permanent marker to trace different-size circles on the plastic file folders. Cut the circles out and place them on top of the light box.

STEPS

1. Allow your toddler to explore the primary color circles on top of her new light box.

2. Encourage her to move them around and notice the new colors they make when the colors overlap and the light shines through. Help her identify the colors, if needed.

3. Add more learning by helping her put them in order according to size from smallest to largest. Show her how they can stack on top of one another to make neat circular designs.

TIP *Cut other shapes out of translucent folders to expand on the learning and creativity.*

CAUTION! *Never leave the lights on for long periods of time or after play. Supervise your toddler during play, and never leave the activity set up when not supervising, as the materials used can be a strangulation or injury hazard.*

Squishy Shape Friends

Add a squishy sensory experience, beneficial fine-motor-skill practice, and lots of imagination to your toddler's basic shape learning.

Messiness: 2
Prep Time: **None**
Activity Time: **20 minutes**

MATERIALS

Gallon-size plastic zip-top bag

4 permanent markers, each a different color

1 (16- to 20-ounce) bottle translucent hair gel

8 to 12 large googly eyes, various sizes and colors

Duct tape

STEPS

1. Have your toddler review the basic shapes (circle, square, triangle, and rectangle) while you draw each one on one side of the plastic bag using a different colored permanent marker. Add some details to the outside of each shape, such as spiky hair, stick arms, pointy ears, or little legs.

2. Have your toddler hold the bag open while you squirt the hair gel inside. Then let her add the googly eyes. Close the bag and fold duct tape over the zip-top for extra security.

3. Have her help flatten the bag on the table, shapes-side up.

4. Encourage her to poke and squish the bag with her fingers to move googly eyes into each shape to bring it to life. Help her make up silly stories about her new shape friends.

CAUTION! *Monitor your toddler closely when playing with small objects. This activity may not be suitable for children who put objects in their mouths during play. Supervise your toddler during play, and never leave the activity set up when not supervising, as the materials used can be a choking or injury hazard.*

SKILLS
LEARNED

colors

creativity

fine
motor skills

sensory
development

Rainbow Spaghetti Snip & Style

Cooked spaghetti—with some bright colors and scissor practice thrown in for good measure—makes great sensory bin fun for toddlers who like to explore with their mouths during play.

MATERIALS

1 (16-ounce) box spaghetti

Stove, saucepan, and spaghetti server

6 medium plastic food-storage containers, with tight lids

Water

Measuring spoon

6 teaspoons cooking oil

6 teaspoons vinegar

Food coloring, in red, orange, yellow, green, and blue

Colander

Large shallow plastic bin

Marker

White paper

Safety scissors

Messiness: 3
Prep Time: 15 minutes + 1 hour dyeing time
Activity Time: 20 minutes

PREP

1. Cook the spaghetti, according to the package directions, but about two or three minutes *less* so it remains al dente (firm to the bite).

2. While it's cooking, fill each food-storage container halfway with water, a teaspoon of oil, a teaspoon of vinegar, and 10 to 15 drops of food coloring, using a different color for each container.

3. When the spaghetti is done, drain it in a colander and run cold water over it until cool. Divide it equally among the six containers and then secure the lid on each one.

4. Have your toddler help shake each container to disperse the color. Allow the spaghetti to sit in the containers for an hour or so before draining each one in the colander and rinsing with cold water to remove excess dye.

5. Add each color of spaghetti to the plastic bin,, in a row in rainbow order.

6. Use the marker to draw a large simple smiley face on a piece of paper and place it next to the bin.

STEPS

1. Invite your toddler to explore the colorful spaghetti in the bin with his hands.

2. Demonstrate how to use safety scissors to snip the spaghetti and allow him to do some snipping. Encourage lots of color identification during play and spaghetti snipping.

3. Have your toddler arrange their snips of spaghetti on the paper to make a colorful hairdo on the smiley face.

CAUTION! *Keep your toddler away from the stove and hot ingredients. Supervise your toddler during play, and never leave the activity set up when not supervising, as the materials used can be a choking hazard.*

early literacy   fine
motor skills   sensory
development   shapes
and letters

Salty ABCs

Help your little one practice writing the letters of the alphabet in a sensory-rich way that he's sure to love.

Messiness: 2
Prep Time: None
Activity Time: 20 minutes

MATERIALS

Large plastic tray, or shallow plastic bin

Salt

Foam bath letter toys

STEPS

1. Together with your toddler, cover the inside of the tray with a thin layer of salt.

2. Place the foam letter "A" next to the tray and have your toddler trace over it with his finger.

3. Demonstrate how to write the letter in the salt with your finger. Have your child trace over it with his finger. Then, give the tray a wiggle to erase the letter and have him try writing it in the salt on his own.

4. Wiggle the tray again and repeat, for each letter of the alphabet, or as long as your child has interest. Once he's got the hang of it, have him write the letters on his own without demonstration or tracing.

TIP *If your tray is white or light in color, line it with a bright color of construction paper, using tape, as needed.*

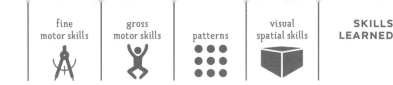

Sticky Zigzag Patterns

This easy-to-implement activity will surely keep your little one occupied for a while. Plus, she'll be using fine and gross motor skills.

Messiness: 3
Prep Time: None
Activity Time: 20 minutes

MATERIALS

Painter's tape

Sticky notes, in 2 or more colors

STEPS

1. Discuss what a zigzag line is while making a long one on the floor with painter's tape.

2. Demonstrate for your toddler how to stick sticky notes on the line, one after another and edge to edge.

3. Allow her to stick sticky notes down, covering the entire zigzag line.

4. Add to the learning by challenging her to make simple patterns along the lines using the different color sticky notes, such as an ABA pattern (*pink, blue, pink . . .*) or an ABBA pattern (*pink, blue, blue, pink . . .*).

TIP *Customize the learning by making shapes, letters, or numbers on the floor instead.*

SKILLS
LEARNED

fine
motor skills

sensory
development

visual
spatial skills

Sticker-Match Sensory Bin

Use stickers related to your child's interests to make this sensory-filled matching game even more fun.

Messiness: 3
Prep Time: 10 minutes
Activity Time: 20 minutes

MATERIALS

8 pairs of matching stickers

8 plastic bottle caps

Construction paper

1 (2-pound) bag rice

Medium plastic bin

PREP

1. For each sticker pair, place one sticker on the top of a bottle cap and the other on the construction paper.

2. Add the rice to the plastic bin and bury the sticker-topped bottle caps in the rice. Place the construction paper next to the bin.

STEPS

1. Have your toddler dig through the rice in the bin with his hands to find a bottle cap.

2. When he finds a cap, have him place it on its matching sticker on the paper.

3. Repeat, until all caps and stickers have been matched.

CAUTION! *Monitor your toddler closely when playing with small objects. This activity may not be suitable for children who put objects in their mouths during play.*

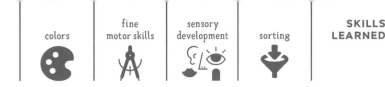
Feather Surprise Sort

This color-sorting activity incorporates the thrill of anticipation with the silky feel of feathers, which little fingers love.

Messiness: 2
Prep Time: 5 minutes
Activity Time: 10 minutes

MATERIALS

Craft feathers, various colors

Large empty tissue box

Construction paper, 1 sheet per feather color

Tape (optional)

PREP

1. Add the feathers to the tissue box.

2. Place one sheet of paper matching each feather color, in a row or large rectangle, next to the tissue box. If you're playing on the floor, tape the paper down for safety.

STEPS

1. Invite your toddler to reach into the tissue box and take out just one feather.

2. Have her identify the color and place it on its matching paper.

3. Allow her to repeat, pulling and sorting each feather onto its matching-color paper.

TIP *Count the feathers on each color of paper when you're done for some extra learning.*

SKILLS
LEARNED

language development

listening

sensory development

shapes and letters

Foamy Mirror Fun

Get your little one creating and talking about different types of lines and shapes in a super sensory way.

Messiness: 4
Prep Time: None
Activity Time: 10 minutes

MATERIALS

Bath towel

Large mirror

Shaving cream

Hand towel

STEPS

1. Spread the bath towel out on a table, place the mirror on top, and spray shaving cream on the mirror. Allow your toddler to smooth it out with his hands. Keep the hand towel nearby for cleaning little hands and the play area, as needed.

2. Encourage your child to draw different lines (swirly, wavy, zigzag, straight, etc.) and shapes (circle, square, triangle, rectangle, etc.) on the foamy mirror with his finger.

3. Help him identify or describe the lines and shapes while doing so.

4. Add to the fun and learning by playing a game of follow-the-leader, where you draw a line or shape, and then he draws a matching one next to it.

TIP *No mirror to lay on the table? Try this on an upright mirror. Just put towels on the floor underneath to catch the mess.*

CAUTION! *This activity may not be suitable for children who may put their hands in their mouths during play. If you have never used shaving cream during play, test it on a small area of your toddler's skin beforehand.*

SKILLS
LEARNED | fine
motor skills | numbers and
counting

123 | sorting | visual
spatial skills

Sort & Clip Card Games

Setup doesn't get easier than gathering clothespins and playing cards. With these two items, your toddler will be working those fingers while practicing sorting, numbers, and counting.

Messiness: 2
Prep Time: **None**
Activity Time: **10 minutes**

MATERIALS

Playing cards

10 clothespins

4 medium plastic food-storage containers or a large divided plastic tray (optional)

CAUTION! *Monitor your toddler closely when playing with small objects.*

STEPS

Use the deck of playing cards and other household materials for the following activities:

1. **Suit Sort:** Identify each suit in the deck (hearts, diamonds, clubs, and spades). Place one of each in a different section of the tray. Have your toddler sort the remaining cards onto their matching suit cards in the tray.

2. **Number Sort:** Identify each number in the deck (2 through 10). Place one of each on the table in sequential order. Have her sort the remaining cards onto their matching number cards.

3. **Number Order:** Place one card of each number, randomly, on the table. Challenge her to rearrange them in sequential number order.

4. **Number Cover:** Have her identify the number on the card before covering the number with a clothespin. Repeat with each card, practicing hand-eye coordination.

5. **Number Clip:** Review the numbers in the card deck, then spread the cards out randomly on the table. Call out random numbers for her to find on the cards and clip with the clothespin.

6. **Count & Clip:** Challenge her to clip the number of clothespins around the edge of the card based on the number on the card. Remove the clothespins and repeat with another card.

Rainbow Ring Threading

Threading beads onto string is an important developmental task for toddlers, but it can often be quite challenging for little fingers. Try making the activity pieces bigger for your toddler.

Messiness: 2
Prep Time: 10 minutes
Activity Time: 20 minutes

MATERIALS

Scissors

5 to 10 cardboard tubes

Colored tape, or markers, in red, yellow, orange, green, blue, and purple

Painter's tape

Lightweight play scarves, or wide ribbon, in red, yellow, orange, green, blue, and purple

Basket

PREP

1. Cut the cardboard tubes into one- to two-inch rings.

2. Use colored tape to mark the outside of each ring with a color of the rainbow. No need to cover the entire ring perfectly as long as it's easily identifiable by your toddler.

3. Tape one corner of each scarf down, side by side, on the floor.

STEPS

1. Give your child the color rings in a basket and help him identify the different colors.

2. Challenge him to pick a ring, identify its color, find the matching-color scarf, lift the free end, and thread the ring onto it toward the taped end.

3. Repeat, sorting and threading each color ring onto its matching-color scarf.

CAUTION! *Keep your toddler away from the scissors during prep.*

SKILLS
LEARNED

numbers and
counting

social-emotional
development

visual
spatial skills

123

"Measure Me" Craft Sticks

Older siblings or friends might already know how to use a ruler, but they'll still have fun helping introduce your toddler to basic measuring, using just craft sticks and their bodies.

Messiness: 1
Prep Time: None
Activity Time: 20 minutes

MATERIALS

Craft sticks

Household objects
and furniture

STEPS

1. Demonstrate how to measure with craft sticks: Have your toddler lie on the floor. Make a line of craft sticks, end to end, on the floor next to her, starting at the bottom of her feet and ending at the top of her head. Have her get up off the floor and, together as a group, count the sticks in the line on the floor.

2. Allow the kids to repeat step 1, measuring one another with the craft sticks.

3. Encourage them to use the craft sticks to measure various objects and furniture around the house.

TIP *Experiment with using other household objects for measuring, such as sticky notes or plastic spoons.*

Fuzzy-Circle Exploration

Pom-poms are always a fun sensory material for little fingers. When my kids were little, I discovered a way to add more fuzzy circles to their pom-pom play.

Messiness: 3
Prep Time: 10 minutes
Activity Time: 15 minutes

MATERIALS

Pipe cleaners, in 2 or 3 colors that match the pom-pom colors

Scissors

Pom-poms, various colors

Medium shallow plastic bin, or plastic tray

PREP

1. Use various lengths of pipe cleaner to create different-size circles, twisting ends and trimming or wrapping them back around the circles, as needed.

2. Place the fuzzy pipe cleaner circles and pom-poms into the bin.

STEPS

1. Invite your child to explore the fuzzy pom-poms and circles in the bin. Help him identify the colors.

2. For interactive play, hold a fuzzy circle up and have him put a matching-color pom-pom through the circle.

3. For independent play, arrange various pipe cleaner circles on a flat surface and have him find and place a matching-color pom-pom inside each circle.

TIP *Color matching isn't required. The pom-poms and circles are also simply fun to explore and use to create designs on a tray or table.*

CAUTION! *Keep your toddler away from sharp materials during prep. Monitor your toddler closely when playing with small objects. This activity may not be suitable for children who put objects in their mouths during play.*

SKILLS
LEARNED

fine
motor skills

oral motor
development

shapes
and letters

visual
spatial skills

Laundry-Basket Alphabet Pop

Get those foam letters out of the tub and use them to entertain and educate your toddler.

Messiness: 2
Prep Time: **None**
Activity Time: 15 minutes

MATERIALS

Plastic, slotted laundry basket

Foam bath letter toys, or craft foam shapes

STEPS

1. Help your toddler sit in the laundry basket and put the foam letters in her lap.

2. Have her choose a foam letter and help her identify it.

3. Encourage her to slide the letter through one of the slots in the side of the basket, saying "Pop!" as it goes through.

4. Repeat, with one letter at a time for the entire alphabet.

5. When all letters are outside the basket, choose one at a time, without her seeing which, and slide them back through with a "Pop!" each time one goes through. Help her identify each letter as it falls inside.

TIP *If your toddler can't sit in the laundry basket, just flip it over to push letters through the sides that way. If your basket doesn't have large enough slots for the foam letters, try smaller craft foam letters or shapes instead. Use other shapes or numbers to enhance learning and interest.*

Stormy Sensory Bottle

Sensory bottles are a great toddler-calming toy. The heavy weight helps regulate the sensory system and watching the sparkly storm move inside the bottle inspires mindfulness. Plus, making one with your toddler is a fun activity when it's too stormy to be outside.

Messiness: 2
Prep Time: **None**
Activity Time: **20 minutes**

MATERIALS

1 (6-ounce) bottle glitter glue, in silver or blue

1 (8-ounce) empty clear plastic water bottle, label removed

Water

Sequins, in silver and blue

Craft glue

STEPS

1. Squeeze the glitter glue into the plastic bottle. Fill it the rest of the way with water.

2. Have your toddler help put the sequins in the bottle. Then add some craft glue around the lid threads before tightening the lid on the bottle.

3. Encourage her to shake it to disperse the glitter glue and sequins throughout the water.

4. Help her notice the glitter storm and sequin raindrops swirling and falling inside.

TIP *Offer the sensory bottle for your child to shake and watch when she needs to calm her "stormy emotions" or body.*

CAUTION! *Helping make the sensory bottle may not be a suitable activity for children who put objects in their mouths during play.*

Recyclable Impressions

Making playdough impressions is fascinating for toddlers. Squishing objects into the dough offers lots of sensory and fine-motor-skill work. And seeing the impression each object makes in the dough offers an element of surprise.

Messiness: 3
Prep Time: None
Activity Time: 20 minutes

MATERIALS

Recycled materials, such as plastic bottles, squares of cardboard, jar lids, and plastic containers

Medium plastic bin

Playdough (recipe on page 116 or store-bought)

STEPS

1. Have your toddler help gather various recycled materials from the recycling bin and put them into a plastic bin, choosing ones that are toddler friendly; skip glass, metal, and too-small bottle caps.

2. Invite him to use the recycled materials in the bin to press and squish impressions into the playdough.

3. Encourage him to notice and describe the shapes and lines made, such as straight lines from the edge of the cardboard, circles from jar lids, and a flower shape from the bottom of a plastic water bottle.

Basic Playdough Recipe

MATERIALS

2 cups flour

1½ cups salt

2 tablespoons cream of tartar

Mixing bowls and spoon

1 to 2 tablespoons cooking oil, any type

1 to 2 cups warm water

Make homemade playdough with your toddler by adding the dry ingredients to a mixing bowl and stirring them to combine.

Add the wet ingredients to a separate bowl and stir to combine.

Finally, slowly add the wet ingredient mixture to the dry ingredients, stirring to combine until a dough starts to form and pulls away from the sides of the bowl. Have your toddler knead the dough until it reaches a soft, nonsticky playdough consistency. Knead in more flour or water, as needed.

Hello! Goodbye!

Family pictures add so much fun and learning to this easy activity. You can practice family members' names, family relationship titles, and saying "Hello!" and "Goodbye!"—while getting beneficial hand-eye coordination practice.

Messiness: 1
Prep Time: 5 minutes
Activity Time: 20 minutes

MATERIALS

Heavy-duty scissors or utility knife

Empty canister with a lid, such as a baby formula canister or a container of oats

Tape (optional)

Construction paper or scrapbooking paper (optional)

Black permanent marker (optional)

10 to 20 photos of family members

PREP

1. Use scissors or a utility knife to cut a slit in the canister lid. Make sure it's wide and long enough for the photos to slide through.

2. If you have time and want to save the activity, use tape and paper to cover the outside of the canister. Use a permanent marker to write "Hello!" on one side and "Goodbye!" on the other.

STEPS

1. With the lid on the canister, have your toddler choose a photo, identify the family member(s) and their relationship titles (dad, sister, grandma, uncle, etc.), and then slide the photo through the slit in the canister while saying "Goodbye, [title/name]!" For example, "Goodbye, Uncle Tom!"

2. Have her repeat this until all the photos are inside the canister.

3. Help her remove the lid, reach in, and take a random photo out while saying "Hello, [title/name]!" Have her repeat this for each photo.

TIP *This is a great use for all the family photos sent to you throughout the holiday season.*

CAUTION! *Keep your toddler away from sharp materials during prep.*

Count & Feed Friend

Practicing shapes, colors, and counting will be super fun when making this little tissue-box friend. But be sure to use tongs so no one gets their fingers "nibbled!"

Messiness: 3
Prep Time: 5 minutes
Activity Time: 20 minutes

MATERIALS

Scissors

Empty tissue box

Duct tape, any color

Self-adhesive googly eyes

Stickers (optional)

Craft foam shapes or construction paper cut into small shapes

Kitchen tongs or kid's plastic tweezers

CAUTION! *Keep your toddler away from sharp materials during prep. Monitor your toddler closely when playing with small objects. This activity may not be suitable for children who put objects in their mouths during play.*

PREP

1. Use scissors to remove any plastic from the opening of the tissue box, if needed.

2. If the tissue box has a distracting design, cover it (or at least the top of it) with duct tape, leaving the opening uncovered.

STEPS

1. Invite your toddler to bring the tissue box to life by sticking googly eyes above the box's opening. Have him decorate the rest with stickers, if desired. Have him name his new box friend.

2. Together, use the foam shapes to review basic shapes and colors. Explain that this new friend loves eating shapes and colors and is hungry!

3. Call out specific numbers, shapes, and colors for him to feed the box friend, counting and feeding the shapes, one at a time, into the mouth opening using tongs. For example, "Our friend is so hungry for three circles." "Those were yummy! Now she wants four green rectangles."

4. Add listening and memory practice by giving more complex number, shape, and color combinations. For example, "Now our friend is *really hungry* and wants one red rectangle, one blue circle, and one green triangle."

Scoops, Funnels & Shapes

One simple addition made out of cardboard adds shape learning and lots more fun to a simple scoop-and-funnel sensory activity.

Messiness: 3
Prep Time: 10 minutes
Activity Time: 30 minutes

MATERIALS

Cardboard

2 shallow plastic bins, 1 large and 1 medium

Marker

Heavy-duty scissors

Utility knife

Tape

2 (42-ounce) containers old-fashioned oats

Scoops and funnels, various sizes

CAUTION! *Keep your toddler away from sharp materials during prep. Monitor your toddler closely when playing if they put objects in their mouths during play.*

PREP

1. Make a cardboard lid for the medium-size bin by tracing the top of the bin on the cardboard using the marker. Then cut the lid shape out using scissors.

2. Use a utility knife to cut two- to three-inch holes out of the cardboard lid. Make each hole a different basic shape (circle, square, triangle, rectangle, diamond, etc.).

3. Tape the cardboard lid onto the top of the medium-size bin, along only one edge, so it is hinged.

4. Place this lidded bin inside the larger bin (to contain any mess). Pour the oats into the larger bin, and add the funnels and scoops.

STEPS

1. Invite your child to explore the oat-filled sensory bin as well as the medium-size bin inside.

2. Encourage him to experiment with using the funnels in the shape holes for scooping oats into the lidded bin.

3. Challenge him by calling out certain shapes for him to locate and use the funnel to scoop oats through it.

TIP *No oats? Use any small, dry, pourable material you have on hand, such as dried split peas or rice.*

Large-Scale Texture Lacing

Who needs lacing cards when you've got a laundry basket? Give your little one practice lacing on a large scale and use materials of different textures for extra sensory fun, too!

Messiness: 2
Prep Time: 5 minutes
Activity Time: 20 minutes

MATERIALS

Fiber materials, various textures, such as wide ribbon, rope, cord, twine, or even lightweight play scarves

Scissors

Medium basket or bin

Laundry basket, with slots or holes

Painter's tape (optional)

Craft sticks (optional)

TIP *Add color learning by using wide ribbon in each color of the rainbow. Then call out certain colors for her to find and lace.*

PREP

Cut the fiber materials into various two- to three-foot lengths and place them in a basket.

STEPS

1. Invite your toddler to explore the fiber materials in the basket. Discuss their textures using words like *soft, scratchy,* and *bumpy.*

2. Demonstrate how to hold the end of a material and lace it in and out of the holes on the side of the laundry basket.

3. Allow her to try, choosing materials from the basket and lacing them in any way she wants through the sides of the basket.

4. Allow her to discover how the end of a material will go all the way through when lacing. Problem solve together to come up with a solution, such as tying the end in a knot, tying the end to the basket, or taping the end to the basket.

5. If she struggles to lace the materials through the holes, tape a craft stick on the end for her to use like a needle.

CAUTION! *Keep your toddler away from sharp materials during prep. Supervise your toddler during play, and never leave the activity set up when not supervising, as the materials used can be strangulation and injury hazards.*

Sticky Snowstorm

Is it too cold to go outside? Keep your toddler busy exploring textures and expanding his creativity by creating a snowstorm of his own indoors.

Messiness: 3
Prep Time: 5 minutes
Activity Time: 30 minutes

MATERIALS

Tape

Clear contact paper

White, gray, and silver materials, such as tissue paper squares, cotton balls, cotton swabs, snowflake-shaped sequins, silver rhinestones, crinkle paper filler, or strips of newspaper

Large divided plastic tray

PREP

1. Tape a large square of contact paper, sticky-side out, onto a window or wall.

2. Place various white, gray, and silver materials in the divided tray.

STEPS

1. If you have snow outside, take a moment to have your toddler look out the window and discuss what he sees.

2. Invite him to feel the sticky contact paper and show him how the materials from the tray stick to it. Have him use the materials from the tray on the sticky contact paper to make a sticky snowstorm.

3. After some time for unguided discovery and creativity, show him how to stick cotton swabs in a snowflake pattern on the sticky snowstorm.

CAUTION! *Monitor your toddler closely when playing with small objects. This activity may not be suitable for children who put objects in their mouths during play. Never leave the activity set up when not supervising, as the materials used can be a choking hazard.*

colors

sorting

visual
spatial skills

**SKILLS
LEARNED**

Beach Towel Block Mosaic

This easy indoor activity only uses a couple everyday items: building blocks your toddler already plays with and a colorful beach towel.

Messiness: 2
Prep Time: **None**
Activity Time: **20 minutes**

MATERIALS

Large colorful beach towel

Painter's tape

Wooden and/or plastic building blocks, various colors

STEPS

1. Spread the beach towel out on the floor, taping down each corner for safety. Help your child identify and point to the different colors on the towel.

2. Invite her to place building blocks on their matching colors on the towel. Encourage her to cover the entire towel.

TIP *Add to the fun by finding other colorful toys or objects around the house, such as letter magnets or pom-poms, to add to the beach towel mosaic.*

- 6 -
BRING THE OUTDOORS IN

You might not be able to get outside, but you can definitely bring the outdoors in. Each activity in this chapter helps you and your toddler explore the outdoor world and its natural wonder. Some activities incorporate actual natural objects into the play, while others have a clever nature or weather theme. Either way, these indoor-play ideas will have you and your little one celebrating the great outdoors while staying comfortable inside.

SKILLS
LEARNED | fine
motor skills | problem-
solving | science | sensory
development

Nature Surprise!

This easy nature-focused guessing game offers lots of fine-motor-skill practice, hands-on learning, and the exciting element of surprise.

Messiness: 2
Prep Time: 5 minutes
Activity Time: 10 minutes

MATERIALS

Various natural objects, such as stones, small sticks, pine cones, seashells, and acorns

Aluminum foil

Basket

PREP

Wrap each natural object in foil, until fully covered, and place them in a basket.

STEPS

1. Have your child touch and explore the foil-wrapped objects in the basket. Explain how they are natural objects and then explain the difference between natural and man-made by saying something like, "Natural objects and materials come from nature: plants, animals, or rocks. Man-made materials are what people make out of natural ones by changing them."

2. Invite him to choose an object, feel it for a moment, and try to guess what natural object it is before unwrapping the foil to find out.

3. Repeat, inspecting, guessing, and unwrapping each natural object.

CAUTION! *Monitor your toddler closely when playing with small objects. This activity may not be suitable for children who put objects in their mouths during play.*

SKILLS
LEARNED

early literacy

fine
motor skills

imagination

language
development

social-emotional
development

Mini Nature World

Have you and your toddler dabbled in small-world play yet? Even if you've never heard the name, she may have already started playing this way, or likely will soon. During small-world play, a child uses small objects and toys to set up lifelike environments and play out real-life stories, in miniature. Entice your toddler with some nature-filled small-world play when she can't be outside in nature herself.

Messiness: 4
Prep Time: 5 minutes
Activity Time: 20 minutes

MATERIALS

Natural materials, such as grass clippings, pebbles, acorns, stones, pine cones, leaves, and small twigs

Glass vase filler gems, rhinestone gems, or large sequins, clear and/or blue

Large divided plastic tray

Large shallow plastic bin

Plastic food-storage containers, various sizes (optional)

Fabric scraps, old towels, or rags, in earth tones of blue, green, or brown

Playdough (recipe on page 116, or store-bought)

Small toy animals and/or figures

PREP

1. Place a natural material or a gem in each of the divided sections of the tray.

2. Place the large bin on the floor and the other materials around it.

STEPS

1. Invite your child to explore the natural materials. Identify and discuss each one.

2. Together, create a mini nature world inside the large bin. Try these easy ideas:

   - Place upside-down containers in the bin and drape them with fabric or towels to make mountains and valleys.
   - Position large rocks and stones as hills and boulders.
   - Arrange gems or sequins into lakes, rivers, or streams.
   - Use small bits of playdough on the bottom of the bin to hold pine cones or twigs up like trees.
   - Sprinkle grass clippings for toy animals to eat or rest in.

3. Allow her plenty of time for imaginative play with toy animals or figures in her mini nature world. Ask questions and offer prompts to encourage storytelling and language development.

CAUTION! *Monitor your toddler closely when playing with small objects. This activity may not be suitable for children who put objects in their mouths during play.*

Sparkly Snow Soup

Most toddlers are just itching to get out and play in the snow when they see those flakes start to fall. But for various reasons, it's not always possible. On snowy days like that, I would sometimes surprise my kids by bringing snow inside!

Messiness: **4**
Prep Time: **5 minutes**
Activity Time: **20 minutes**

MATERIALS

Towels

Large and medium plastic bins

Snow

Mixing bowls, measuring cups, and spoons

Winter gloves

Glitter

PREP

1. Line the floor or surface with towels and place the large bin on top.

2. Fill the medium bin with snow from outside and place it inside the large bin.

3. Add various mixing bowls, measuring cups, and spoons inside the large bin, also.

STEPS

1. Place the large bin on the towel-lined surface or floor. Then put some gloves on your toddler and allow him to explore the snow.

2. Encourage him to make "snow soup" using various bowls, measuring cups, and spoons to scoop, measure, mix, and stir the snow. Help him sprinkle glitter in his snow soup, if desired.

3. Encourage him to notice when the snow starts to melt and turn to water.

CAUTION! *Monitor little fingers to make sure they don't get too cold playing for long periods in the snow.*

Family Photo Tree

The next time you're playing outside, take your toddler on a nature hunt for a branch to use for this rainy day craft project. She'll get meaningful time with you and you'll get a wall hanging to treasure forever.

Messiness: 3
Prep Time: None
Activity Time: 30 minutes

MATERIALS

Branch, clean and free of leaves

Decorative tape, in various patterns or colors

Scissors (optional)

Medium plastic bin (optional)

5 (2- to 3-foot-long) pieces of ribbon, various colors

Clothespins

Family photos, printed

Hanging hardware

Twine

STEPS

1. With the branch on the floor or another flat surface, have your toddler decorate it with small pieces of decorative tape. You can cut or rip tape pieces and lightly stick them onto an upside-down bin to make it easier for her.

2. Tie one end of each ribbon onto the branch, about equal distances apart.

3. Help your toddler use clothespins to clip the family photos randomly on the ribbons. Identify the people in each photo and describe what you each love about them.

4. Use hanging hardware and twine to securely hang your family tree branch on the wall, horizontally and with the ribbons and photos hanging down from the branch.

TIP *If you have time and want a more colorful tree, have your toddler help glue each photo onto colorful paper using a glue stick. Trim around each one, leaving a half-inch border, and add them to the tree.*

CAUTION! *Supervise your toddler during the activity, and never leave the activity set up when not supervising, as the materials used can be a strangulation or injury hazard. When hanging the branch, make sure it is secure from falling and high enough to be out of reach of your toddler.*

imagination

language
development

sensory
development

Bathtub Beach Party

When you can't get to the beach, bring the beach to your toddler—with some fun beach gear and real seashells to explore, of course.

Messiness: 2
Prep Time: 5 minutes
Activity Time: 20 minutes

MATERIALS

Bathtub and water

10 to 20 seashells

Toy ocean animals

Kids swim ring, inflated

Scissors

1 yellow craft
foam sheet

4 to 5 blue craft
foam sheets

Toy beach pail,
strainer, and shovel

Beach towel

Beachwear, such
as swimsuit, beach
hat, sunglasses,
and snorkel

PREP

1. Fill the bathtub about halfway with water. Add the seashells, the toy ocean animals, and the swim ring.

2. Use scissors to cut a sun out of the yellow craft foam. Then cut ocean waves along one long edge of each sheet of blue craft foam. Tape the foam sun up high on the bathtub wall. Get the foam waves wet in the bathwater and stick them on the wall around the bathtub.

3. Place the beach pail, other beach toys, and a beach towel beside the bathtub.

STEPS

1. Dress your toddler in his beachwear and head to the bathroom. Share in his excitement when he sees the bathtub beach!

2. Help him into the bathtub and with putting on the swim ring, if desired.

3. Encourage him to use the beach pail, strainer, and shovel to search for and explore seashells and toy ocean animals. Help him identify and discuss each as he discovers them.

4. Let him reposition the foam waves around the bathtub, too.

CAUTION! *Supervise your toddler during water play, and never leave the activity set up when not supervising, as the materials used can be a choking, drowning, or injury hazard.*

Farmer Jane's Fields

My parents bought a poultry farm when I was a toddler. Much of my early childhood was spent alongside my hardworking mama—and twenty thousand chickens, a few beef cows, one sweet calf named Curly, and my pet pig, Mortimer (who quickly outgrew any pet potential). Now, I'm no "Farmer Jane," but I want my kids to understand and appreciate where their food comes from. Foster an appreciation for agriculture in your toddler, too, with some farm-themed play!

Messiness: **4**
Prep Time: **5 minutes**
Activity Time: **20 minutes**

MATERIALS

Large shallow plastic bin

Construction paper, in shades of green, brown, and black

Tape

Playdough (recipe on page 116, or store-bought)

Various small natural materials, such as split peas, black beans, popcorn kernels, sunflower seeds, and small pieces of hay

Large divided plastic tray, or another large tray

Toy tractors

PREP

1. Line the inside bottom of the bin with differently colored sheets of construction paper, using tape as needed.

2. Place the playdough and a different small natural material in each section of the divided tray.

STEPS

1. Invite your toddler to bring her tractor toys to the farmer's fields inside the bin.

2. Help her identify and touch each natural material in the tray. Discuss how farmers plant seeds to grow crops, like grains and vegetables.

3. Challenge her to plant some crops in the field using the playdough and natural materials. Encourage imaginative play with the toy tractors throughout.

4. After some free time for play and discovery, help her make long snakes of playdough and press them onto the paper fields for squishing and planting natural materials in.

5. Add to the learning by encouraging her to make patterns in the fields by varying rows of crops or natural items in a row.

CAUTION! *Monitor your toddler closely when playing with small objects. This activity may not be suitable for children who put objects in their mouths during play. Supervise your toddler during play, and never leave the activity set up when not supervising, as the materials used can be a choking or injury hazard.*

Sand & Seashells Name-Find Bottle

Make an easy spy bottle for your toddler to practice the letters in his name, while exploring sand and seashells.

Messiness: 2
Prep Time: **10 minutes**
Activity Time: **20 minutes**

MATERIALS

Sand

Measuring cup

3 plastic food-storage containers, 1 large and 2 small

Small seashells

Letter beads, A–Z

1 (20-ounce) empty clear sports drink bottle, label removed

Funnel (optional)

Craft glue

Black permanent marker

CAUTION! *This activity may not be suitable for children who put objects in their mouths during play.*

PREP

1. Place the sand and a measuring cup for scooping in a large container.

2. Add the seashells and letter beads each to a small container.

STEPS

1. Help your toddler look for the letter "A" in the container of letter beads, and then put it in the empty bottle. Repeat, looking for "B," and so on, for each letter of the alphabet.

2. Have him add the seashells to the bottle. Encourage him to inspect each one while doing so.

3. Using the funnel and measuring cup, if necessary, scoop sand into the bottle until it's about three-quarters full. Add craft glue to the threads inside the cap before tightening it on.

4. Use the permanent marker to write your child's name along the side of the bottle. Say each letter and read his name aloud while doing so.

5. Give him the bottle to move and shake to find each letter of his name, using the name written on the side as a guide.

TIP *This craft offers your toddler fine-motor-skill work and letter practice. But if you're worried about the mess or his safety, make the bottle during naptime or after bedtime to surprise him when he wakes up!*

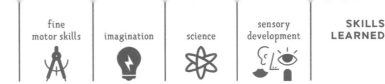

Ice Road Trucker

My toddler nephews love all things with wheels. Have a little one who likes wheels, too? Invite her to explore the changing properties of ice with a fun icy road activity in the sink!

Messiness: 3
Prep Time: 5 minutes + freezing time
Activity Time: 20 minutes

MATERIALS

1 (9-by-13-inch) baking pan

Sink and water

Stepstool, or dining chair

Toy trucks

1 (16-ounce) box sugar cubes

Shaker of salt

TIP *If possible, have your toddler help with prep so she can see the before and after of the water and ice.*

PREP

Add about two inches of water to the pan and place it outside if it's cold enough or in the freezer, until frozen.

STEPS

1. Help your toddler stand safely on a stepstool positioned in front of the sink. (Stay nearby for assistance and safety.) Place the pan of ice inside the sink and run warm water over it to loosen the ice. Carefully remove the rectangle of ice from the pan and place it in the bottom of the sink. Set the pan aside.

2. Invite your child to explore the ice with her hands and the toy trucks. Provide sugar cubes to line the sides of roads or to haul in toy trucks.

3. Sprinkle salt on the roads, as salt trucks would, and help her notice any changes to the ice.

4. Discuss how the water turned to ice when it got cold and is melting back to water as it warms up. Use ice-related words like *cold, freezing, slippery, melting*, and *water*.

CAUTION! *Supervise your toddler during play, and never leave the activity set up when not supervising, as the materials used can be a slipping and injury hazard. Always stay nearby when your toddler is standing on a stepstool or chair.*

Petal Pluck & Count

Allow your toddler some up-close observation of flowers while strengthening fine motor skills, hand-eye coordination, and number learning.

Messiness: 2
Prep Time: **5 minutes**
Activity Time: **10 minutes**

MATERIALS

Marker

12 paper baking cups

12-cup muffin pan

6 to 12 flowers (wildflowers or store-bought)

Magnifying glass (optional)

Kid's plastic tweezers, or other tweezers (optional)

PREP

1. Use the marker to write a number, 1 through 12, on the inside bottom of each paper baking cup.

2. Place the numbered baking cups in numeric order in the cups of the muffin pan.

STEPS

1. Allow your child to examine the flowers. Provide a magnifying glass, if possible, to look closely. Discuss how they look, smell, and feel.

2. Review the numbers, 1 through 12, in the muffin pan cups.

3. Have him use his fingers or tweezers to pluck and place petals in each muffin pan cup, using the numbers in the cups as a guide for how many to put in each.

TIP *Flowers you've had in the vase for a while will be easier to pluck than freshly cut flowers. If you have flowers of different colors, use markers to color the inside bottoms of the paper baking cups with matching colors. Then have your toddler pluck and sort petals by color.*

Color-Block Leaves

Explore autumn leaves and their various colors with your toddler by making a color-block collage while you're warm and cozy inside.

Messiness: 3
Prep Time: 5 minutes
Activity Time: 20 minutes

MATERIALS

Construction paper, 1 sheet each of red, yellow, orange, and green

Painter's tape

Clear contact paper

Leaves, various colors

Opaque paper or plastic grocery bag

PREP

1. Arrange the four sheets of different color construction paper into a two-by-two square on the floor. Lightly tape them down.

2. Tape clear contact paper, sticky-side up, over the paper on the floor so that you can see the paper colors through it. If you need to use two rows of contact paper, overlap it a bit so they stick together.

3. Place leaves in a bag your toddler cannot see through.

STEPS

1. Help your toddler identify each color of the color-block design on the floor. Allow her to explore the stickiness, too.

2. Have her reach in the bag without looking inside and pull out a leaf. Encourage her to examine the leaf and identify its color, then stick the leaf on its matching-color block.

3. Repeat until the entire color-block collage is covered, or as long as she has interest.

TIP *If you want to keep your color-block leaves collage, add more clear contact paper, sticky-side down, over the top, and trim the edges.*

Artsy Indoor Snowman

Wait until you see the excitement in your toddler's eyes when you tell him that he is going to make a snowman inside!

Messiness: **3**
Prep Time: **None**
Activity Time: **20 minutes**

MATERIALS

Winter gloves

Snow

Medium plastic bin

3 nesting mixing bowls

Large shallow
plastic bin

Craft gems (optional)

Paintbrush

Washable paint

STEPS

1. Together with your child, put on gloves. Gather snow from outside, put it into the medium bin, and bring it indoors.

2. Keeping the gloves on, help him use the mixing bowls like molds to make three domes of snow in graduated sizes, like a snowman's shape, along the bottom of the large bin.

3. Encourage him to press gems into the snowman for eyes, nose, mouth, and buttons. Allow him time to get creative and paint the snowman using a paintbrush and paint. And, of course, encourage more fancy gems for decoration.

4. After he's done, extend the learning by checking the bin every so often to observe and discuss how the artsy snowman melts.

TIP *If you're not interested in observing the snowman melt, use the colorful fancy snow in the bin for sensory play, similar to Sparkly Snow Soup on page 130.*

CAUTION! *Monitor your toddler closely when playing with small objects. Skip the gems if your child is likely to put small objects in his mouth. Supervise your toddler during play, and never leave the activity set up when not supervising, as the materials used can be a choking and injury hazard. Monitor little fingers to make sure they don't get too cold playing for long periods in the snow.*

SKILLS LEARNED

creativity

fine
motor skills

sensory
development

visual
spatial skills

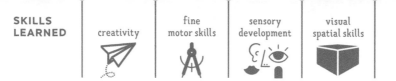

Scented Pumpkin-Dough Village

This pumpkin-spice-scented playdough brings the pumpkin fun indoors when the autumn weather starts getting colder.

Messiness: **4**
Prep Time: **5 minutes**
Activity Time: **20 minutes**

MATERIALS

Black permanent marker

3 to 6 mini pumpkins and gourds

1 to 2 tablespoons pumpkin pie spice

Playdough (recipe on page 116, or store-bought)

Cinnamon sticks

Pumpkin seeds (optional)

Small plastic bowl (optional)

PREP

Use the permanent marker to draw square and rectangle windows and doors on the sides of the mini pumpkins and gourds.

STEPS

1. Add the pumpkin pie spice to the playdough, fold it over, and knead a couple times to get it started. Ask your toddler to help knead it. Add small amounts of oil, as needed, until the dough reaches the desired consistency.

2. Allow free time for her to build and create a village with the playdough, pumpkin and gourd houses, cinnamon sticks, and pumpkin seeds.

3. Encourage her to try building taller by squishing playdough between stacked pumpkins and gourds.

TIP *If you're making a new batch of playdough, add the pumpkin pie spice during the dry ingredients step.*

CAUTION! *Although the homemade pumpkin playdough is taste safe, it is not fully edible.*

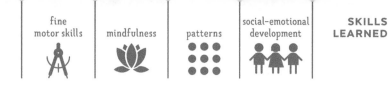

Seeds & Beans Spiral

Get your little one practicing his thumb and finger pincer grasps along with mindfulness and focus while making a calming spiral design using only seeds, beans, and one other common household item.

Messiness: 2
Prep Time: **None**
Activity Time: 10 minutes

MATERIALS

Pen

Foam plate

Small bowl of sunflower seeds

Small bowl of dried beans

STEPS

1. With the pen's point retracted or the cap on, draw a spiral on the plate, leaving an impression in it but no ink. Have your toddler use his finger to trace over the spiral impression and explain how spiral lines like this sometimes help people feel calm and focus their attention.

2. Have him start at the outside and place seeds and beans side by side along the spiral line. The impression will help them stay in place. But encourage him to focus and use mindful (or slow and careful) movements.

3. If he's up for it, challenge him to try an AB pattern (*seed, bean, seed, bean...*) along the spiral. Then, try an ABBA pattern (*seed, bean, bean, seed...*) along some of it.

CAUTION! *Monitor your toddler closely when playing with small objects. This activity may not be suitable for children who put objects in their mouths during play.*

fine
motor skills

imagination

science

sensory
development

Grow & Style Fairy Hair

Let your little one explore seeds and learn about plant growth with this whimsical spin on a grass hair activity.

Messiness: 3
Prep Time: None
Activity Time: 30 minutes

MATERIALS

Self-adhesive
googly eyes

White disposable cup,
foam or paper

Flower stickers

Sparkly pipe cleaners

Craft glue or tape

Black permanent
marker (optional)

Soil and water

Wheatgrass, chia, or
cress seeds

Safety scissors

STEPS

1. Have your toddler put two googly eyes on one side of the cup.

2. Invite her to decorate the bottom half of the cup with lots of flower stickers.

3. Help her bend the pipe cleaners into fairy wings and glue them on the back of the cup.

4. Add a mouth and other details to the cup with a permanent marker, if desired.

5. Have your child help fill the cup with soil and then plant and water the seeds according to the package directions.

6. Observe and discuss the fairy hair growth each day. When it has grown tall enough, allow your toddler to style the fairy's hair by snipping it with safety scissors. Just make sure she knows to never cut her own hair.

CAUTION! *Monitor your toddler closely when playing with small objects. This activity may not be suitable for children who put objects in their mouths during play.*

Lightning Bug Hunt

Growing up in the country made catching lightning bugs (or fireflies, as some call them) a regular activity. Make some cute little lightning bugs with your child to use for a lightning bug hunt right in the house!

Messiness: 1
Prep Time: **None**
Activity Time: **30 minutes**

MATERIALS

Plastic beads, black, yellow, and gold

Up to 5 sparkly pipe cleaners

5 circles of white tissue paper, using a 2- to 3-inch jar lid for tracing

Scissors

1 (40-ounce) clear plastic peanut butter jar with lid, empty and clean

Black permanent marker

STEPS

1. Have your toddler help thread a black bead onto a pipe cleaner, for the lightning bug's head. Then help him twist the pipe cleaner around itself to secure the bead at one end.

2. Accordion fold a circle of tissue paper and pinch it in the center to make wings. Twist the pipe cleaner around the paper to attach the wings just behind the black bead.

3. Have your child thread four or five yellow and/or gold beads onto the pipe cleaner behind the wings. Twist the end of the pipe cleaner around itself behind the last bead to secure them and finish your lightning bug. Trim the pipe cleaner, if needed.

4. Repeat steps 1 through 3 to make four more lightning bugs.

5. Use the permanent marker to write the word "bugs" on the side of the jar. Help your toddler identify the letters and read the word to him as you do so.

6. Have him cover his eyes while you hide the lightning bugs around the house. Then send him on a lightning bug hunt, collecting them in his jar as he finds them.

TIP *You could prep steps 1 and 2 ahead of time so the lightning bugs are ready for your toddler to simply thread beads on. Or, if you're not up for crafting lightning bugs, hide yellow pom-poms around the house as lightning bugs instead.*

CAUTION! *Monitor your toddler closely when playing with small objects. This activity may not be suitable for children who put objects in their mouths during play.*

SKILLS
LEARNED

imagination

oral motor
development

sensory
development

social-emotional
development

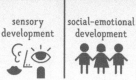

Animal-Sound Orchestra

Bring outdoor wildlife inside with this creative group game full of animal-sound fun! It's silly enough to reset the lulling mood on a long day indoors.

Messiness: 0
Prep Time: **None**
Activity Time: **10 minutes**

MATERIALS

None

STEPS

1. If there are five or fewer kids, have them sit in a row on the floor. If there are more, have them sit in a circle.

2. Explain that they will each be an instrument in the orchestra (or a large group of musicians playing different instruments together), but there is a catch—the instruments make animal sounds!

3. Have each child choose a different animal sound. Help little ones, as needed.

4. Tell them they can only play their animal instrument (make the sound) when the conductor (the person who directs when to play) taps them on the head.

5. Be the conductor for the first round by tapping the kids randomly on the head, having them make their sound when tapped. Adjust the speed of your tapping to make the animal-sound music sillier and the game more fun.

6. Allow each child to have a turn being the animal-orchestra conductor. Revel in the giggles!

Window Weather Observer

My kids always had their noses to the windows when the weather kept us in. They were fascinated with everything happening outside. Here's a fun activity to harness your toddler's curiosity while adding some practice in visual perception and language skills.

Messiness: 1
Prep Time: None
Activity Time: 20 minutes

MATERIALS

Washable markers

Nature- or weather-themed stickers

2 (4½-inch) cardboard tubes

Decorative tape, any color or pattern

Window

STEPS

1. Have your toddler use the washable markers and stickers to decorate the outsides of the tubes.

2. Help her position the tubes together like a pair of binoculars, and then tape a few times around them both to hold them together.

3. Invite your child to use her binoculars to observe the weather and nature outside the window. Encourage her to use descriptive words to describe what she sees.

4. Play a simple "I Spy" game by taking turns calling out objects for the other to find with the binoculars.

SKILLS
LEARNED

fine
motor skills

imagination

sensory
development

Dirty Slime Construction Site

Making slime was my J.C.'s favorite activity to do alongside his big sister, Priscilla. Let's just say their slime making is *not* clean indoor fun. However, proper materials and a few tricks can turn slime making with your toddler into an easier, little-bit-cleaner activity. Plus, the sensory experience, fine-motor-skills benefits, and plain old fun are worth it!

Messiness: **4**
Prep Time: **None**
Activity Time: **30 minutes**

MATERIALS

1 (3.9-ounce) box chocolate instant pudding mix

1 cup cornstarch

Mixing bowl and spoon

Warm water

4 to 8 chocolate graham crackers (optional)

Sandwich-size plastic zip-top bag (optional)

Toy dump trucks and construction equipment

Large shallow plastic bin

STEPS

1. Help your toddler add the pudding mix and cornstarch to the mixing bowl and stir to combine.

2. Add the warm water a couple tablespoons at a time, stirring continuously, until the mixture pulls away from the sides of the bowl and forms a slime.

3. Let your toddler knead and explore the slime mixture. Add more water or cornstarch, as needed, to adjust the consistency.

4. Have your child use his fingers to crush the graham crackers inside a sealed zip-top bag.

5. Invite him to play pretend construction site with the graham cracker crumbs, dirty slime, and his toy dump trucks and construction equipment inside the plastic bin. Encourage lots of scooping, hauling, and tire-track fun!

TIP *Skip the graham cracker crumbs for less mess.*

CAUTION! *While this slime is taste safe, it isn't fully edible.*

Hanging Rainbow Suncatcher

Is the sun shining but it's too hot to play outside? Regardless of the reason you can't go outside to play, you can make this colorful suncatcher with your toddler to celebrate the sun.

Messiness: 1
Prep Time: **None**
Activity Time: **30 minutes**

MATERIALS

Double-sided tape

6 clear plastic party cups

Small tissue paper squares, in each color of the rainbow: red, orange, yellow, green, blue, and purple

Scissors

1 (3-foot) string

3 jingle bells

CAUTION! *Supervise your toddler during play, and never leave the activity set up when not supervising, as the materials used can be a choking and strangulation hazard.*

STEPS

1. Apply double-sided tape every half inch or so around the outside of a cup. Have your toddler press red and orange tissue paper onto the tape to cover the entire cup. Slide another cup over it, sandwiching the colorful tissue paper between the two.

2. Repeat, using yellow and green tissue paper for one set of the remaining cups and blue and purple tissue paper for the other set.

3. Use scissors to carefully poke a hole through the center of the bottom of each pair of cups.

4. Have your toddler help thread a jingle bell onto one end of the string. Tie it at the end. Help him thread the other end through the hole in the blue-purple cups, from the inside, and pull it all the way through until the bell is inside the cups.

5. Repeat, tying another bell about six inches up the string and threading on the yellow-green cups. And repeat again, with the red-orange cups.

6. Use the remaining end of the string to hang the colorful-cup suncatchers near a window, but safely out of your child's reach. Encourage your toddler to notice the light shining through the suncatchers.

Colorful Pine Cone Wrap

Gather some pine cones with your toddler when you have some time outside. Then you'll have them ready for this easy, colorful activity on the next rainy day indoors.

Messiness: 1
Prep Time: None
Activity Time: 20 minutes

MATERIALS

Pine cones, clean and dry

Yarn, multiple 1- to 2-foot lengths of various colors

TIP *It might be helpful to start the string once around the pine cone before having your toddler continue wrapping.*

STEPS

1. Have your toddler inspect the pine cones while you discuss them. Use a simple explanation, such as, "Pine cones hang on pine trees and hold the tree's seeds in their scales. Then, when the seeds are ready, they open their scales to let the seeds fall to the ground so they can grow into more trees."

2. Have her choose a piece of yarn and identify the color. Then have her choose a pine cone and show her how to decorate it with the yarn, pressing it between the scales while wrapping it around multiple times. Allow her to try, using another piece of yarn, if needed.

3. Have your toddler repeat, wrapping each pine cone in yarn. Allow her to be creative and choose any colors of yarn. Or have her wrap each in just one color and use them for color identification and play.

CAUTION! *Monitor your toddler closely when playing with small objects. This activity may not be suitable for children who put objects in their mouths during play. Supervise your toddler during play, and never leave the activity set up when not supervising, as the materials used can be a choking and strangulation hazard.*

SKILLS
LEARNED

early literacy

imagination

listening

social-emotional
development

Teddy Bear Camping

It might be too cold or rainy to go camping outside, but that doesn't have to stop you from having some camping-themed fun inside—with teddy bears!

Messiness: 2
Prep Time: 10 minutes
Activity Time: 30 minutes
(or all night!)

MATERIALS

Play tent, or sheets, large clips, and dining chairs to make one

Pillows and blankets

Battery-powered camping lanterns and flashlights

Camping-themed children's books

8 to 10 (3-inch) craft foam squares, in tan and dark brown

Cotton balls

2 large plastic storage containers

Teddy bears and other stuffed animals

Construction paper, gray

Battery-operated LED candles

Tissue paper, in red, orange, and yellow

Tape

PREP

1. Set up a play tent in the living room. Place pillows, blankets, camping lanterns, flashlights, and camping-themed children's books inside.

2. Place the craft foam squares and a couple handfuls of cotton balls in a container near the tent.

STEPS

1. Invite your toddler to gather some teddy bears and join you at the campground!

2. Have her help build a pretend campfire on the floor by crumpling gray construction paper into pretend stones, arranging them in a circle, placing the lit battery-operated candles in the circle, and then covering the candles with an upside-down container. Cover the container with torn and crumpled tissue paper, using tape, as needed, to make flames.

3. Gather with your toddler and her teddy bears around the campfire. Discuss campfire safety while you pretend to warm your hands.

4. Have her follow your directions to make a pretend s'more. Use one tan foam square as a graham cracker, one brown foam square as a piece of chocolate, one cotton ball as a marshmallow, and another tan foam square as a graham cracker on top. Hold it like a sandwich. Encourage her to repeat, making pretend s'mores for her teddy bear friends.

5. Dim the lights and have your child and her teddy bears join you in the tent. Show her how to shine a flashlight at her hands to make shadow puppets on the tent wall. Or use some printable camping-themed shadow puppets via the link in the Resources section on page 157.

6. Turn the lantern on and snuggle up to read some books together.

CAUTION! *Supervise your toddler during play, and never leave the activity set up when not supervising, as the materials used can be an injury hazard. This activity may not be suitable for children who put objects in their mouths during play.*

Resources

ACTIVITY PRINTABLES

Find printable resources for the following activities at B-InspiredMama.com /rainy-day-toddler-activities-resources.

- Phone Number Song Fun (page 43)
- Color Taste Test Picnic (page 48)
- Indoor Penny Yard Sale (page 52)
- Mini Home Office (page 60)
- Dress Up Dice (page 61)
- Teddy Bear Camping (page 154)

CHILDREN'S BOOKS

Little Blue Truck by Alice Schertle and Jill McElmurry

This cute truck- and farm-animal-themed story was read so often to my kids when they were toddlers that I can still recite the entire thing 10 years later. Pair it with Farm Animal Roundup (page 70) or while using toy trucks on the Twist & Turn Track (page 77).

Outside Your Window: A First Book of Nature by Nicola Davies and Mark Hearld

Pair this sweet poetry book about nature with Window Weather Observer (page 149) or any of the nature-themed activities in chapter 6 (page 125).

The Little Snowplow by Lora Koehler and Jake Parker

This little storybook about a small but mighty snowplow is the perfect addition to the indoor snowplow fun of Snowplow Rider (page 83).

The Rainbow Fish by Marcus Pfister

An ocean-themed book would make your pretend play even more magical (and educational) during the Under-the-Table Sea activity (page 54).

TouchThinkLearn: ABC by Xavier Deneux

Books with interactive and tactile elements like this one often help capture the attention of wiggly toddlers. Pair this simple alphabet book with any of the letter learning activities, such as Alphabet Balloon Ball (page 87) or Salty ABCs (page 102).

Katie and the Starry Night by James Mayhew and Lee Wildish

Grab this children's book for when you do the Magical Starry Sky art project (page 32). Katie will take you and your toddler on an up-close journey through some of Vincent van Gogh's most famous and stunning paintings.

Swirl by Swirl: Spirals in Nature by Joyce Sidman and Beth Krommes

The striking illustrations throughout this book about spirals found in nature make it one of my very favorites. It would make the perfect book to read just before the calming Seeds & Beans Spiral activity (page 143).

RESOURCE BOOKS

The Outdoor Toddler Activity Book: 100+ Fun Learning Activities for Outside Play by Krissy Bonning-Gould

The companion book to this rainy day book, written by me! Lots of fun and educational toddler activities for outside play, no matter the weather or the season.

Play & Learn Toddler Activities Book: 200+ Fun Activities for Early Learning by Angela Thayer

Here's another helpful book you'll want to have handy through the toddler years. Written by my blogging mama friend, Angela Thayer (founder of Teaching Mama), *Play & Learn Toddler Activities Book* is the forerunner that inspired this book and its outdoor activities predecessor. As a former teacher and fellow mama of three, she has tons of experience and expertise in child development, hands-on learning, and, of course, play!

150+ Screen-Free Activities for Kids: The Very Best and Easiest Playtime Activities from FunAtHomeWithKids.com by Asia Citro

This mama knows kids and fun! Asia Citro—a blogging friend, founder of Fun at Home with Kids, and author of multiple kids' activities books and an award-winning kids' chapter book series, *Zoey and Sassafras*—has you covered when it comes to entertaining, educating, and connecting with your kids. Check out her outdoor activities book, *A Little Bit of Dirt: 55+ Science and Art Activities to Reconnect Children with Nature*, too.

The Slime Book by Stacey Garska Rodriguez and Jennifer Tammy Grossi

If you and your little one had fun with the slime making and play in this book (on page 150), you'll love *The Slime Book*'s slimy fun and recipes. My dear friends Stacey and Jennifer have developed, mixed, stretched, tested, and even sometimes tasted hundreds of slime recipes to find 40 that won't disappoint.

100 Fun & Easy Learning Games for Kids: Teach Reading, Writing, Math, and More with Fun Activities by Amanda Boyarshinov and Kim Vij

Full of games and activities to make learning fun, this book—by two of my long-time blogging pals, Amanda and Kim—will be one you come back to over and over throughout the years. While most of the activities have a preschool focus, many can be modified for toddlers, too.

First Art for Toddlers and Twos: Open-Ended Art Experiences by MaryAnn F. Kohl

My former-art-teacher heart loves everything MaryAnn Kohl writes. This book, in particular, focuses on inspiring little ones to experience and learn through making art. Process over product always!

99 Fine Motor Ideas for Ages 1 to 5 (Volume 1) by Nicolette Roux, Laura Marschel, Blayne Burke, Georgina Bomer, Devany LeDrew, Sarah McClelland, Kristina Couturier, Dyan Robson, Emma Craig, and Samantha Soper-Caetano

This book is loaded with clever and creative fine-motor-skill activities for toddlers and preschoolers. From busy bags to craft projects to DIY toys, you're sure to find a fine-motor-skill-strengthening activity your toddler will love!

WEBSITES & BLOGS

Busy Toddler: BusyToddler.com

Susie shares tons of quick and easy toddler activities with a focus on fun, hands-on learning. She tries to ensure each activity has no prep or less than five minutes of prep so real moms can actually implement them.

Hands On As We Grow: HandsOnAsWeGrow.com

Jamie Reimer has amassed an extensive resource for moms and caregivers on her blog promoting hands-on play and learning activities. Not only does her blog have thousands of free ideas, but Jamie also offers helpful activity plans in ebooks and a monthly membership called *The Activity Room.*

Teaching 2 and 3 Year Olds: Teaching2and3YearOlds.com

Sheryl Cooper is an experienced toddler and preschool teacher who shares all of her tried-and-tested early learning ideas on her blog. But her ideas aren't just for the classroom; they're simple enough for any busy mom to pull off, too.

Teaching Mama: TeachingMama.org

Angela Thayer uses her years of teaching experience to develop fun learning activities that toddlers and preschoolers love. Plus, she authored the popular toddler activity book *Play & Learn Toddler Activities Book: 200+ Fun Activities for Early Learning.*

Toddler Approved: ToddlerApproved.com

Kristina has been sharing fun and creative activities for little ones for years. She aims for each activity to foster creativity and a love for learning.

References

Hassinger-Das, Brenna, Kathy Hirsch-Pasek, and Roberta Michnick Golinkoff. "The Case of Brain Science and Guided Play: A Developing Story." *Young Children* 72, no. 2 (May 2017). Accessed December 7, 2018. www.naeyc.org/resources/pubs/yc/may2017/case-brain-science-guided-play.

HealthyChildren.org. "Ages & Stages: Toddler." Accessed October 6, 2018. www.healthychildren.org/english/ages-stages/toddler/Pages/default.aspx.

Pathways.org "Toddler Milestones." Accessed October 6, 2018. www.pathways.org/growth-development/toddler/milestones.

Index

Acknowledgments

Just as raising a child takes a village, so too does writing a book while being a mom!

Thank you to my friends at Callisto Media for seeing potential in me and B-Inspired Mama, and for providing me a bridge to other mamas and caregivers. Susan, thank you especially for your patience and support while I (often clumsily) juggled this project with motherhood.

This book would never have come to be if not for my number one cheerleader, dinner preparer or takeout picker-upper, super-fun dad, and *magical* husband, Clifford Gould II. Thank you for teaching me how to love better, including how to better love myself.

My gratitude also to my parents, Tammy and Raymond Sherman. The values you instilled in Josh and me, and that you still exemplify, of commitment, responsibility, perseverance, family, and love, are roots that nourish every idea and accomplishment. Speaking of Josh, I'm so thankful to have a brother with such a caring, goofy heart who has given me an incredible sister, cool niece, two adorable nephews, and thoughtful advice whenever I ask (but not when I don't).

This mama is grateful for her mama friends, too! Thank you, Michele Clark, for years and years of support and encouragement. You're an incredible mother, person, and friend. And thank you, Katie Mitchell, for listening, laughing, understanding, and praying.

A note of gratitude to my former husband, now friend, Brian Bonning, for helping me bring two incredible kids into this world, loving them so much, and navigating this crazy coparenting journey alongside me.

My three children are the true authors of this book, as they are the authors of my mama heart. Sawyer, Priscilla, and J.C., your creativity, wonder, kindness, and love fuel everything I do. Thank you for your patience when I hid behind my laptop in the living room or stressed about deadlines. I hope you can look back someday and appreciate how important and impactful it was to share your mommy with her creative work. You are world changers.

I cannot leave out my B-Inspired Mama supporters. Whenever you use even one of my ideas to love on your children or students, my heart fills with hope and joy. Thank you for the hard work you do for children and the world.

About the Author

KRISSY BONNING-GOULD is a former art teacher with a master's degree in K–12 art education turned full-time blogging mama. She is also the author of *The Outdoor Toddler Activity Book: 100+ Fun Early Learning Activities for Outside Play*. Upon becoming a mom, Krissy founded B-Inspired Mama as a creative outlet; however, it ignited a passion within her for blogging and helping fellow moms. Over the past 10 years, between pregnancies and playdates for her children, Sawyer, Priscilla, and J.C., Krissy immersed herself in blogging, social media, and content marketing to grow B-InspiredMama.com into an extensive resource for kids crafts, learning fun, kid-friendly recipes, and creative parenting. Follow her fun via email at B-InspiredMama.com/subscribe, on Twitter and Instagram by following @BInspiredMama, and online at Pinterest.com/BInspiredMama, Facebook.com / BInspiredMama, and Facebook.com/SensoryActivitiesforKids.